D0911793

BOOK SOLD
NO LONGER R.H.P.L.
PROPERTY

Où vais-je vivre?

Rosemary McCarney

Texte français de Valérie Bourdeau

Éditions
📖 SCHOLASTIC

Parfois, des choses effrayantes arrivent à de braves gens.

RICHMOND HILL PUBLIC LIBRARY
32972000370728   RG
Où vais-je vivre?
Jun. 08, 2017

Hongrie

Quand des soldats se battent ou que des dangers surviennent,

Rwanda

les familles doivent plier bagage et chercher
un endroit où vivre en sécurité.

Elles partent en voiture,

à pied,

Hongrie

ou au pas de course, dans l'espoir de trouver un endroit sûr.

Hongrie

Mais moi? Où vais-je vivre?
Est-ce que ce sera au bout de cette route?

Au-delà de cette colline?

Slovénie

Derrière cette grille?

De l'autre côté de l'océan?

Soudan du Sud

Vais-je vivre sous un tapis?

Sous un escalier?

Grèce

Dans une tente?

Ou dans un campement?

Kenya

Vais-je vivre dans un endroit chaud et sec?

Ou dans un endroit froid et enneigé?

Cameroun

Vais-je me faire un nouvel ami?

Ou même plusieurs?

Hongrie

Vais-je dormir au même endroit chaque nuit?

Liban

Vais-je avoir un nouveau lit rien qu'à moi,
ou vais-je devoir le partager?

Jordanie

Tant de questions... mais aussi tant d'espoir.

Après un si long voyage et une si longue attente…

Niger

j'espère que quelqu'un me sourira et me souhaitera la bienvenue.
J'espère que ce quelqu'un sera toi.

punishment, in her book, *The Perils of School: Cultural Clashes in Communities and Classroom.*

While some may argue that it is not essential to understand the content of the debate surrounding the involvement of African American parents in their children's schooling in elementary and secondary schools to understand college choice, I would suggest that it is crucial to do so because college choice theorists recognize the hugely important role that the family plays in influencing students' postsecondary plans (Hossler & Gallagher, 1987; Hossler, Braxton, & Coopersmith, 1989). The questions underlying both debates, although often unspoken and unwritten, are: Do African American families value education? Do they perceive a return on their investment in higher education? If so, how do they impart this value of education to their children, that is, do their children perceive the same value? In order to understand the context of how African American families influence the college choice process of their children, it is important to first review the value that these families have placed on education over time and in what ways they have passed on their value of education, particularly higher education, to their children. Without such a context, it is difficult to understand the African American family's role in the college choice process.

Overview of African American Families' Belief in Education

Sociologist Billingsley (1992) addressed the quest of African Americans for education often through his writings. As he indicates, "Education is the traditional opportunity through which Black families find their place in life. And having found it, they replicate their experience again and again through their children" (p. 172). Education, in the broadest sense, is fundamental to being able to communicate and to participate in the affairs of society. When any group of people has been denied the right to read and write, as was historically the case with African Americans when their ancestors came to this country, instinctively, they will come to attach a high premium on those skills (Anderson, 1988).

First of all, early on African Americans recognized that they were locked out of the flow of information—there was no way they could adequately navigate their surroundings without the

Part One
Familial and Individual Influences

CHAPTER 1

The Influence of Family

3 1833 04818 9390

Wrongly, African American families are often accuse being involved or interested in the outcome or th tional process of their children. Whether it is participat Parent Teacher Association (PTA) meeting at the element secondary level or assisting students in the transition to education institutions, African American parents are dep uncaring. In fact, a whole body of literature has sprung demonstrate the linkages between community and schoo targeting African American children as not being suc because their parents are not actively participating in the ac of the school.

While no one would doubt or question the importa parental involvement in the schooling process, the findings r ing many African Americans' participation are often skew distorted. Many prominent African American historians and ologists who have written about the African American family discussed the belief of these families in the role and power of cation (Anderson, 1988; Billingsley, 1992; Franklin & Ligh 1989). Perhaps the more recent assessment of findings related lack of African American family involvement in their child schooling points to both a lack of understanding as to how African American family interprets its role and involvement a conflict between the values of the family and the school. Vei Feagans (1997) discusses some of these conflicts, such as styl necessary communication skills. As such, learning the basics of reading and writing became not only a priority but a necessity. Literacy was so important to African Americans that many actually lost their lives when their surreptitious efforts to learn to read and write were discovered. For example, in their report prepared for the Joint Center for Political Studies in 1989, Sarah Lawrence Lightfoot and John Hope Franklin noted, "The desire to learn to read and to write was keen in the Black communities of antebellum America.... Even in the dilapidated log cabins of the slave quarters the desire for education was nurtured and strengthened as an integral part of the socialization patterns and kinship networks of Black men and women held in bondage" (p. ix). The historic commitment African American families had toward education has continued in various ways since slavery. For example, African Americans have continued their fight for education throughout the courts—most notably with the 1954 Supreme Court desegregation decree.

Additionally, the way in which families historically have been involved in their children's education is noteworthy. Education has always been a matter of interest for the entire family and community. The church, the extended family (including grandparents and other relatives), and the immediate family have always been involved in the education of African American children. The idea continues to be that each generation is to have more opportunities than the generation before it. For example, it is not unusual today to find African American churches "passing the hat" to help with the education of college students. It is not unusual to hear the value of education being discussed in various venues. For instance, a grandmother recently brought her grandson to my barber shop for a haircut. While we were waiting to get our hair cut, several other young African American men came in. The latest drug bust was being discussed on the evening news on television. The grandmother started to lecture the young men. She said, "You see, our future is left to you boys, and in order to make it, you're going to need education. It's the only way."

However, when researchers write about the education of African American students and their families today, they most often point to decaying families. The Lightfoot panel addressed this issue in 1989 by stating the following: "What we must demand is this: that the schools shift their focus from the supposed deficiencies of the Black child—from the alleged inadequacies of Black family life—to the barriers that stand in the way of academic success" (p. ix).

While committed early on to the basics of education, African American families have nonetheless been interested in their childrens' involvement in higher education, as seen in the establishment of HBCUs, which were founded between 1830 and 1900 with the very mission of educating African Americans. Since many HBCUs, such as Fisk University, were extension schools, it was not unusual to find entire family members studying side by side. The story of Booker T. Washington stands as an example of African Americans' desire for higher education. He walked to school, slept outside at night, and cleaned a floor with a handkerchief to pay for his schooling (Washington, 1989). While today more African Americans attend PWIs, HBCUs are still producing a disproportionate number of graduates. In sum, as Billingsley stated, African Americans have always had "a deep historical and cultural belief in the efficacy of education. Blacks have sought education in every conceivable manner and at every level" (p. 181). What has not been understood is the way African American families have influenced their children's college choice process.

Factors that Influence the College Choice Process

Although in phase one (predisposition) of the Hossler and Gallagher (1987) model the influence of family is discussed, it is submerged under "significant others." Because the influence of the family differs within each cultural group, there is a need to explicate this role as it relates to African Americans. Although, as Hossler and Gallagher indicate, parents "play an important role in shaping attitudes toward higher education and action toward college choice" (p. 211), how that influence is shaped based on different cultural characteristics needs greater understanding. The way in which African American families value education has everything to do with the way they influence their children's college choice process.

While maintaining vestiges from the past and combining elements of a larger middle class, the way in which African American families influence their children's college choice is noteworthy. As Levine and Nidiffer (1996) state about the findings from their student subjects, "[W]hen asked how they came to attend college, each of them told almost the same story" (p. 65). Although the students I interviewed were in different school types and geographic regions, their responses to my questions about college attendance varied little. For these students, across school types, the influence of family often took on an additional dimension. That is, they were influenced by family members not necessarily because a family member had attended college or received a degree, as this literature supports, but because the family wanted the student to achieve beyond the level of other family members. Additionally, students often mentioned themselves as their own motivators. Therefore students identified three factors that influenced their decision to attend college: (1) an automatic expectation in their family; (2) influences beyond the family level; and (3) self-motivation and avoidance of "what I do not want to be" (see figure 1.1). These will be described in the next sections.

Figure 1.1. The Influence of Family on Students' College Choice

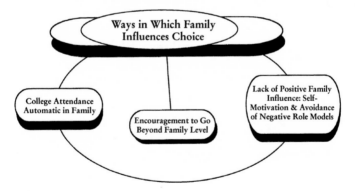

Automatic College Attendance Expectations within the Family

Some students enjoyed automatic support of their educational goals within their family. They were more likely to be students whose parents or some family members were college graduates. One student in a suburban school in Atlanta explained to me, "I didn't even think about not going to college. I knew it was automatic with my family."

A student attending a private school in Chicago had this to say:

> I mean for me, my parents, there was never really a choice for me. I just kind of had to go, and I never really thought about not going, and so going here was just part of the whole thing in going to college.

At another private school in Los Angeles, a student explained,

> It's just been that's what you're supposed to do in my family. I've just been raised on it. My mom has always told me that you go to elementary school, go through junior high and high school, go to college, and pursue your career.

A student at an inner-city school in New York stated,

> [My] family [influenced me]. In my situation I have to live up to expectations. Family members have gone to college, and so it's like, go on and follow the family trend. Just keep going.

This is the category of students that college choice theorists are most familiar with and have written the most about. Theorists have studied students in two categories—those who are high socioeconomic status (SES) and those who are low SES. Presumably, those who are high SES are children of college graduates and are more likely to make college choice automatic. Noteworthy, however, is that students in this category, including those in inner-city schools, can have extended family members who have not attended college and who so influence students' choices that they cannot remember when the desire began.

The ideal scenario for students who are underrepresented in higher education is for there to be a larger number who fall into this category where the idea of choosing higher education is automatic. Unfortunately, the largest number of African Americans participating in higher education are still first-generation college goers and higher education is not automatic. However, with African American families, the value of higher education is often instilled even when family members have not participated in higher education.

Encouragement to Go Beyond the Family's Level of Education

Some African American students reported that their parents or extended family encouraged them (implicitly or explicitly) to go beyond their own level of schooling. Understandably, the responses in this category typically came from students whose parents or family members had not attended college.

For example, a student attending an inner-city school in Chicago said, "My family wants me to go to college because, in my family, I'll be the first one to graduate from high school and also to go to college." Another student attending the same school said, "My grandma is depending on me going on to school." A student attending a private school in Chicago stated,

> Whenever I think about college it's like, my parents, they always wanted me to do better than they did; so...I'll probably be the first one in a long time that ever went to college so I would be something like a role model for my family. That's why I think they want me to go to school—so I'll be able to come out better than how they came out.

At an inner-city school in Washington, D.C., a student explained her mother's influence: "She just talks about how she didn't go and how she couldn't go when she was my age."

The majority of African American students reside in families where there is interest in their participation in and benefitting from higher education. However, students whose parents desire for their children to go beyond their level of schooling because they did not attend college are often limited in their ability to navigate the college choice process. Therefore, substantial resources (financial, informational, and personal) would yield great benefits to this group of students and parents. While college choice theorists would include these parents in the low SES group, the students interviewed made it clear that their parents wanted them to go to college. In order to build on the desires of these parents and students, it is crucial that students in this category of families be provided with appropriate information early so that they do not lose the desire to continue their education. It is logical that this group be targeted for resources since it comprises the largest group of African American families.

Self-Motivation and Avoidance of Negative Role Models

Another theme that could be considered internal to the home is students' indication of themselves as the influence on their perception of the value of higher education. Students in this category usually perceived that there was no family they could rely on for assistance. A student at an inner-city school in New York explained, "I just do everything for myself. Nobody has influenced me." A student at a private school in Los Angeles echoed that response:

> For me, I was my own self motivator because of the area I live in. …I told myself, "Man, you're going to go to high school and you're going to finish it. You're going to go to a university, not city college, and you're going to make something of yourself so you will have something to show for it."

A student at a private school in Chicago responded similarly:

> For me, one of the reasons why I want to go to college is because I don't have a lot of money without having to go to sell drugs, you know, or do the typical whatever, so that I want to support my family.

At a magnet school in Chicago, a student said,

> My father just sits around the house. I don't want to be like him because he'll have a job and get paid, but all he does is waste his money on things he doesn't need when he could put it back to get another house or things that he really does need. It's wrong.

A student at a suburban school said something similar: "My uncle is a bar room bum. I don't want to be like that."

These responses, while focusing on students' perceptions that the influence on their decision to go to college comes from themselves, also provide a different example of how the family impacts students choosing higher education. That is, even though a family member has not gone to college or does not indicate a desire for a younger family member to go beyond the level of schooling achieved by other family members, this does not mean that these potential students should be written off. On the contrary, these students' responses indicate that they can be motivated to choose higher education in seemingly negative home environments; and in fact, these negative influences can cause them to desire higher education more profoundly than those who take the choice for granted.

Self-motivation is an area that needs greater exploration. The self-motivated students receive the least amount of attention, particularly from a research perspective, and yet could demonstrate the greatest potential. Usually, models to increase participation in higher education for students who are in this category have been based on research in the two previously discussed categories. It is obvious why those models have had minimal effect: the family structures and desires are quite different.

The Influence of Family Beyond Socioeconomic Status

There is no denying the influence of the family on students' college choice. In fact, in the Bateman and Hossler (1996) article, three of the five correlates that they indicate relate to predisposition (students choosing higher education) are familial. Two of the three correlates are socioeconomic factors (family income and parental levels of education) and the third factor is parental encouragement. This chapter demonstrates the importance of going beyond socioeconomic status when examining and understanding the influence of African American families on their children's college choice process.

As indicated in this chapter, there are families across the socioeconomic spectrum that influence their children to pursue postsecondary education. In order to influence the students in homes where parents are not educated or are not financially well off, a more in-depth understanding of the ways these families influence their children is necessary. Given the fact that there are still many African American first-generation college-goers, programs and models should be developed especially for these potential students. The necessary programs cannot be developed based on merely understanding the families' socioeconomic differences. We need to know a great deal more about *how* the families in the lower socioeconomic group influence their children.

This chapter, hopefully, has begun the process of probing more deeply into understanding that process. Chapter 2 further expands on when students begin to make their choices and how the family influences them from the start.

CHAPTER 2

Turning Point: When Decisions are Made

Since the process of deciding to attend college is complex, in order to influence the process it is imperative to better understand when African American students begin to decide that higher education is an option or to reject it as an option. Yet, surprisingly, very little research appears to be conducted on narrowing the window on the age or grade when students are influenced in this important decision.

There is much debate about the age of decision making to choose higher education participation. The debate, however, does not appear to have generated much empirical evidence. It does appear that the federal government, through its GEAR UP program, has concluded that the appropriate time to begin to influence the process is middle school (that is, seventh grade). However, to help us better understand when African American students begin to make the decision to go to college, the students surveyed in this chapter reported on not only at what point they were influenced but how they recall that the event or circumstances associated with a particular period influenced them.

Questions that need to be asked include: (1) What do researchers and educators currently know about the age or grade at which decision making about postsecondary studies begins? (2) Is it possible to better pinpoint when decision making occurs? and

(3) Are there particular events that occur at given ages that influence the decision making, particularly of African American students?

When Decisions Are Made: What Researchers and Educators Have Established

Although Hossler and Gallagher (1987) indicated that the first phase of college choice (predisposition) had received the least amount of attention, over the last several years significantly more research has been conducted on this phase (Bateman & Hossler, 1996; Freeman, 1997; Hamrick & Stage, 1998). Even so, most of the studies on the predisposition phase have not addressed the question of the age or grade when students begin deciding about higher education.

As proposed by the Hossler and Gallagher (1987) three-phase model, the predisposition phase does not take into account when the decision process begins (see figure 2.1). That could account for the lack of research on this question. As figure 2.1 indicates, the emphasis in Hossler and Gallagher's model is on the influence of significant others and school characteristics and activities. Because the emphasis is on school characteristics and activities, it is understandable that most of the research on the predisposition phase has focused on ninth grade and higher because it is in secondary school that students are typically involved in extracurricular activities.

Figure 2.1. Phase One: Predisposition

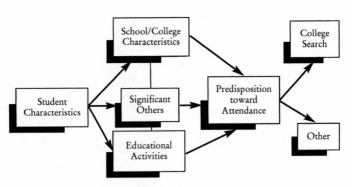

Adapted from Hossler & Gallagher, 1987

However, researchers have concluded that students' decision making concerning higher education occurs before the junior or senior year of high school (Stage & Hossler, 1989). Stage and Hossler, citing Ekstrom, indicated that 61 percent of students had made the decision to attend college or not by the ninth grade. The focus of Schmidt and Hossler's (1995) research was also on the ninth grade as a pivotal point in students' decision making. As such, the majority of their research came from survey data collected by the Indiana College Placement and Assessment Center (ICPAC) of twenty-one high schools in Indiana.

Although most research has focused on the eighth grade and higher, there is beginning to emerge research that questions this timing. For example, Hamrick and Stage (1998) stated, "Researchers have recently speculated that students begin negotiating the college choice process earlier than previously suspected" (p. 345). Drawing on the work of Schmidt and Hossler (1995), Hamrick and Stage indicated that eighth-grade and even seventh-grade students have begun to formulate postsecondary plans. Yet even this speculation of the college choice process beginning as early as the seventh grade does not provide information as to whether this is a critical point during which students may be turned on to or off from considering higher education.

Essentially, then, researchers and educators have focused on grades 7–12 as the pivotal points when, at least, students have finalized their postsecondary education plans. However, as researchers such as Hamrick and Stage (1998) have indicated, those students who have not prepared for higher education participation by grade 7 are at great risk of not choosing college.

While researchers have provided a clue as to the categories of students who choose or do not choose to go to college, they have not matched each category with an approximate age so that appropriate models or programs can be designed. Citing Jackson, Hossler and Gallagher (1987) identified three distinct types of students who emerge in the predisposition phase of college choice:

1. *Whiches:* students who never seriously consider not going to college.
2. *Whethers:* students who apply to one or two local colleges, but may not attend at all.
3. *Nots:* students who never really consider going to college.

According to their report, "[T]he 'nots' identify themselves and pursue noneducational options, the 'whiches' may or may not attend college at all, and the 'whethers' begin to explore postsecondary options" (p. 213).

What makes this model difficult to apply to African American students is, as one principal said to me, that most of these students indicate that they plan to continue on to postsecondary schooling because to say that they do not plan to attend college is like admitting that they are a failure. This principal's insight could account for African Americans having the highest stated college aspirations among all groups. Also because of the presence of HBCUs, African American students may or may not apply to one or two local colleges as in the "whethers"category. For example, as McDonough, Antonio, and Trent (1995) have indicated, California has one of the largest out-migrations of African Americans to attend HBCUs.

Drawing on the distinct types of students identified by Hossler and Gallagher, I would agree that three types of students emerge from the predisposition phase. However, based on the voices of the African American students I interviewed, I propose a different set of distinct types:

1. *Knowers:* students who know they will be attending college. They have always known, "like breathing," as one student expressed it to me.
2. *Seekers:* students who come to believe "I can do this" and begin to prepare and seek information about higher education.
3. *Dreamers:* students who believe that higher education is not an option but may dream about the possibilities.

What separates these distinct categories from the previous model is that African American students of any type may emerge to choose postsecondary education and sometimes do, yet the proposed model leaves room for those students from all three categories who may not choose to participate in higher education. It is therefore possible from this model to better differentiate the pivotal points (ages or grades) that separate the seekers and dreamers and to determine when to instigate programming to impact students' decision making.

The primary difference in the models, then, is that the Jackson model is rigid and does not account for the dynamicism and fluidity that occur in the higher education decision-making process. The model I propose also allows for better consideration of at least a band around the ages and grades during which students, particularly in categories 2 and 3, begin to consider higher education.

At What Age Are Students Influenced in Their Decision-Making Process?

A question that I often pose to African American students, not just to students in the study I conducted, is when did they begin thinking about higher education? It is amazing how well students can pinpoint not only the age or grade when they began considering higher education but also the particular environment, circumstances, or individuals attached to the time period that so inspired them that they have committed it to memory. What is so vital to understanding the age when students begin creating the idea of higher education as an option is that it can not just help establish the most appropriate programs or models to encourage them, but it can help to establish with more specificity when the programs should begin. Relative to the categories of students who consider higher education participation, the following ages should be considered.

Knowers: "Like Breathing"

Like all students, whether by influence of education, socioeconomic level of their parents, or type of school attended, some African American students cannot pinpoint a time when they began thinking higher education was an option because they have always known they would attend. One student in this category said that the decision to go to college was so natural that it was "like breathing." A student attending a suburban school in Atlanta stated, "I didn't think about not going to college." This student's comment supports the description of "whiches" that Hossler and Gallagher (1987) cited. One of his fellow students made a similar comment that captures the importance of environmental influences on the decision process: "I've grown up in this environment so there is really no doubt that I'm going to college." Students in this category usually come from those families in which it is automatically assumed that the students will go to college (see chapter 1).

Also noteworthy is that some parents, particularly of African American students, even when they were not college graduates, still instill the desire "like breathing" into their children. A student attending a private school in Chicago, speaking about his parents who were not college graduates, stated, "For me, my parents, there was never really a choice for me. I just kind of had to go, and I never thought about not going." Another student attending the same school said her mother told her, "You're going to go here and you're going to go to college."

It is obvious that students in this category generally choose postsecondary education. The most important characteristic about students in this category, and what sets them apart from students in the other two categories, is that they begin from a place of strength because they have always known that they would go to college. As such, these students have more information at their disposal to make decisions, better choices of schools (curriculum and activities), and more time to focus on planning phase 2 (the selection process) of the three-phase model set out by Hossler and Gallagher (1987).

Seekers: "I Can Do This"

Aside from students who are knowers, obviously the students who are seekers stand the best chance of opting for college. Surprisingly, the students in this category who were included in the study were able to pinpoint grades 1–5 typically as points when they knew they could "do it"—make higher education an option. This age and grade period is critical because during this time educators have the best opportunity to influence students who do not know, either by birthright or environmental circumstances, that higher education is an option. It is still early enough to provide students the opportunity to take advantage of the information and planning necessary to prepare for higher education.

The way that students in this category described when they began considering higher education and how their consideration was influenced is revealing. For example, a student attending a magnet school in Los Angeles indicated that she had known "since I was age six." In response to what influenced her, she stated, "Well, really my mother. Like when I used to go to Marine World and really liked the animals." In fact, it appears that, in general, seekers are either influenced by family who most likely have not attended higher education or school officials (teachers or counselors) and sometimes the media, as some students indicated. The family members in this group tend to fall in the category of those who encourage the students to go beyond their own level of schooling (see chapter 1). A student attending an inner-city school in Washington, D.C., indicating that her mother "talks about how she didn't go and how she couldn't go when she was my age," said, "I started thinking about it when I was nine or ten."

Sometimes students in this category discuss how at a particular age peers more directly influence them, particularly peers who are older and who have already gone on to college. For example, a student attending the same school in Washington indicated this:

> I started thinking about it in elementary school, and I would hear the older kids when they [would] come home from college talk about it more, and I always wanted to go someday.

Another student, attending another inner-city-school in Washington, indicated how she was influenced at age thirteen by the work of her friend's mother: "I decided when I was about thirteen [that] I wanted to be a nurse. My friend's mother is a nurse. She took me to work with her one day, so I decided."

Two students attending the same inner-city high school in Chicago described when they began considering higher education very differently. One of the students said, "about the age of maybe ten." In her case, she described the media (television) as the influence on her thinking:

> It's like a lot of shows that a lot of us see on television that [were] dealing with psychology [which she wanted to study]. I said, you know, "I think I would like to do that someday. I think I could set my mind into something like that."

Now, as she is approaching graduation, she has already determined to go college and has been accepted by a PWI which she plans to attend.

However, aside from family and friends, teachers and counselors seem to have the greatest influence on seekers. As a student attending a magnet school in Washington said, "It was in third grade when my teacher asked me to be in charge when she stepped out. That day I knew I could some day go to college."

As indicated by these students, seekers are those students who someone has provided early responsibilities, such as a teacher or counselor, who have received a spark from a family member or peer, or who have seen something in the media that made them know that they could go to college. Since, according to them, it was in the early grades when they were influenced, there would be ample time for them to prepare and seek ways to overcome whatever obstacles they would encounter. Most importantly, because they would be able to develop the "I can do" attitude early enough, they would be fortified enough psychologically to overcome any periods of self-doubt.

Seekers, as well as the next category to be discussed, dreamers, often have to rely on information and assistance outside of their home (for example, from school teachers and counselors). Therefore, the timing of programs and models is more important with seekers, and they should continue with dreamers. The seekers' decision process stands the greatest chance of being influenced because these students, when caught young enough, can believe that they "can do this" and can be influenced early enough in school to begin the preparation process. Programming has typically been targeted at knowers, who already know they will attend college, or at dreamers who, in most instances, already would have reached a turning point where they begin to perceive that higher education might not be an option.

Dreamers: Higher Education Option or Not?

In response to when he began plans for postsecondary schooling, another student attending the same inner-city high school in Chicago as the senior quoted above indicated the following:

> Well, to be honest, when I first entered high school, the freshman year, you know, I really hadn't [given it any] thought—you know, eighth grade or seventh grade or elementary. But when I came to high school, I [began thinking about] what I was going to do with my life, you know, after high school.

This student would obviously fall into the dreamer category.

Students who are dreamers fall in the range of seventh to twelfth grade before they begin considering whether or not to go to college. These students are at great risk for not seeing higher education as an option. These are the students who often, perhaps deep down inside, dream of doing something better with their lives. However, they have missed the spark that seekers have received from family, peers, or school. Students in this category lack information and direction, and as students have described it, they lose hope. In other words, in addition to the social barriers, these students face psychological barriers (Freeman, 1997). That is, they lose hope or cannot see options beyond high school. For example, a senior attending an inner-city high school in Chicago demonstrated how he might be dreaming of higher education participation but might be at risk of not participating, when he stated:

> I haven't chosen the school because I am still waiting on the SAT scores to come back, but I want to get into business management where you got the computer technology [and] business management because I [have] always wanted my own business, or something, you know, something like that.

Although this student might ultimately go to college, the fact that he has not begun to consider schools makes it all the more difficult for him to gather the necessary information about the process of searching for various higher education institutions and funding.

It should not be assumed that only African American students attending inner-city schools fall into the dreamer category. Students attending magnet schools as well can be in jeopardy of not choosing higher education. A student attending a magnet school in Chicago had this to say:

> I started this year. I wasn't really into school; but now that I feel that I need more things in life, I started realizing that I should further my education; so, I just started my junior year.

Another student attending a magnet school in Los Angeles captures what can happen to students when they do not have adequate information:

> When I [was] thirteen, I wanted to go to college but I couldn't afford it. But just recently [in her senior year] I found out that there is a way for me to go without money.

It is difficult to imagine that between grades 6 and 12 a student would not be able to receive such basic information or assistance with planning the process of higher education participation. Even when late planners see college as an option, regardless of high school type attended, they can be at risk, or at least hampered, by a lack of information. As an example, a student attending a private school in Los Angeles, who indicated that he did not begin thinking about or planning for school until the ninth grade, stated this:

> I'm a senior. I really don't know where I want to go. I applied to numerous colleges. I want to be a pediatrician when I grow up, and I know in order to become that I have to go to college. Hopefully, I [will] get to play basketball wherever I go.

The key is that this student's plans are not solid. Earlier planning could have assisted him in marrying his academic plans with his obvious love for basketball. However, at least in private schools, there are usually structured counseling programs in place that assist students with the selection process. Even so, late planning can cause students to be underprepared and therefore limited in their choices of higher education institution types.

The primary difference between dreamers and seekers is the age at which they consider higher education. First, because dreamers begin late, they have missed early steps in the preparation process. Next, dreamers can often become disenchanted with school, not involved in extracurricular activities, and not adequately prepared to take the appropriate curriculum of college preparatory classes. Finally, dreamers obviously lack the necessary information about the search process and funding. However, it should not be assumed that because students in this age bracket are at risk they should be written off, because many still dream of higher education as an option and, with proper guidance, can make it a reality.

Connecting Age to the Predisposition Phase: A Critical Linkage

A reconsideration of the age when students begin to be influenced to pursue postsecondary education is crucial. It appears that the best chance of influencing students' decision-making process is in elementary school. During this phase of their lives, students are more receptive to possibilities, and they are malleable enough to mold their beliefs in themselves—to believe that they can go to college. It also causes them to place more emphasis on making good grades and setting good study habits, as well as develop self-esteem.

Although schools play a major role in shaping students into seekers (which will be discussed in later chapters), families and peers also are crucial. As pointed out, these students discussed how they were influenced at an early age by their mother's circumstances (what she desired for them), expanding their world by visiting locations such as Marine World which instilled possibilities, visiting work sites of families and friends, and interacting with peers who were already attending college. Similarly, Hamrick and Stage (1998) suggested that by the seventh and eighth grades, many students begin a form of passive searching by virtue of exposure to older siblings and friends.

The implication of the influence of these events and individuals on students' postsecondary plans is clearly that the students have to be introduced to these events at an early age. College choice theorists (such as Hamrick & Stage, 1998) have recently begun to imply that the age when students begin to formulate their college plans is crucial. Therefore, there is a need to rethink the predisposition phase of college choice to include more research to better pinpoint the age when students make the decision to participate in higher education. It is particularly important to understand if and when students reach a turning point in the decision-making process. Based on these students' comments, it appears that middle school, while not detrimental, is not the ideal time to begin programs. Elementary school is a more ideal time when students can be fortified enough to overcome barriers, particularly psychological barriers, as I have noted (Freeman, 1997).

The most ideal programming would be to focus on getting more students to become knowers and seekers and fewer to become dreamers. In order to prevent students from turning away from higher education as an option, programming should begin as early as first grade (age six) and should include family, mentors, friends, and schools.

CHAPTER 3

Gender Issues: The College Choice Process of African American Females and Males

Much has been made of the decreasing number of African American males who participate in higher education. Among the more than fourteen million students enrolled in American colleges and universities in 1994, African American men had the lowest male-to-female ratio when compared to all other ethnic groups (Cuyjet, 1997). Therefore, understanding how African American males and females approach the process of deciding whether to attend college can provide clues, perhaps, as to why females choose higher education participation in greater numbers than males. Questions to be asked include (1) Who or what do African American females and males perceive as the influences on this decision process? (2) If their perceptions of the influences differ, is it the differences in influences that account for the discrepancies in higher education participation of females and males? And (3) How can these students' perceptions of the influences be useful in modeling programs to increase the number of African American males who choose to go to college?

It is particularly important to assess the differences in the influences on the choice process of African American females and males since, as Cuyjet (1997) suggested, one reason for the lack of representation of African American males on America's college campuses is that there are barriers preventing them from ever getting to college in the first place. Comparing the perceptions of the influences on the decision process of females and males could provide clues as to whether there are programs or models that may be useful for increasing participation of African American males in higher education.

Influences on the College Choice Process of African American Females and Males

The differential schooling experiences of males and females have been well documented. For example, an in-depth study by the American Association of University Women (AAUW, 1990) entitled *How Schools Shortchange Girls* documented widespread differences in the education experiences of boys and girls. The study found "compelling evidence that girls are not receiving the same quality, or even quantity, of education as their brothers" (p. 188). Although this study found that girls receive less attention from classroom teachers than boys, it also found differences between the classroom experiences of White girls and African American girls. It was reported in the study that "African American girls have fewer interactions with teachers than do white girls, despite evidence they attempt to initiate interactions more frequently" (p. 190).

The AAUW findings support the research of Irvine (1990), who wrote, "Teachers' verbal feedback statements do vary according to the student's race" (p. 63). On the whole, according to Irvine, a majority of studies "showed that teachers deliver more negative feedback to black students than to white students" (p. 63). However, although African American students receive more negative feedback from teachers, Irvine continued, "Any consideration of the school experiences of black children must take into account the gender of the children" (p. 79). For example, she indicated that academically African American females outperform males and have higher career aspirations in high school. As Irvine concluded, it seems nonproductive to merely state that African American males are more at risk than females. What is needed is a better understanding of how and why African American students receive differential treatment from White students and how and why there is differential treatment between African American females and males.

At least in-depth studies like the AAUW report have examined the differences between schooling experiences of females and males, and Irvine has assessed the differences between the schooling experiences of African American females and males. However, the AAUW report and Irvine encourage further examination of schooling experiences by gender and race. While it is understandable that these differential schooling experiences impact the choices of African American students, studies are lacking that address the differences in the influences on the college choice process of African American females and males. Researchers need to delve into why it is that more African American males fall into the dreamer category.

As previous research demonstrates, most often the choice process of African American females and males has been examined in the aggregate. The little research that compares the influences on the decision of African American males and females concerning higher education has been mixed. For example, Hossler and Stage (1987) found that overall, women in general think more about attending college but receive less family support than males. In a more recent study to examine comparatively the predisposition of African American and White students to pursue higher education, Bateman and Hossler (1996) found that parents' expectations have the strongest correlation with the plans of their children to attend college. They found that student ability had the second highest correlation with college attendance plans, with the exception of African American females, for whom the mother's educational level was second. Other researchers such as Ellsworth (1982) and Tuttle (1981) found that gender has no significant influence on college predisposition.

Relating more specifically to the planning process for African American females and males, Bateman and Hossler (1996) found that females plan to pursue more education than all groups, while males plan the least amount of education. Overall, however, Bateman and Hossler concluded that "in this study, we know considerably less about the development of educational plans among African Americans when compared to White students" and "the results suggest differences in the factors that influence the postsecondary educational aspirations of African American males and females that were not as pronounced between White males and females" (p. 78). The intent of this chapter, then, is to assess if African American females and males perceive the same or different influences on their higher education plans.

Students' Perceptions of Gender Differences

When students were asked whether the way they perceived the influences on the college choice process for African American females and males differed, they offered responses that would be aligned with what college choice theorists have suggested (e.g., Bateman & Hossler, 1996; Hearn, Griswold, Marine, & McFarland, 1995). Yet their responses can add to researchers' and educators' understanding and, perhaps, can provide clues as to how and why African American females and males perceive the influences differently. In line with college choice theorists, African American males and females perceived that females receive more encouragement, yet their perceptions expanded on this notion by indicating that the rationale for this has to do with females filling a double role of being both African American and female and society's fear of African American males. They also perceived that African American males are primarily encouraged to go to college for their athletic ability, while females are encouraged for their academic ability. An area that students generally agreed on was that expectations are higher from every source for African American females.

The students interviewed did not discuss any perceived differences within the family. However, outside the family (that is, in society and in school) they perceived that African American males and females are influenced in very different ways.

"Killing Two Birds with One Stone" or "Scared to Death"

As an example of how students described what they meant by how females are encouraged more because of their being counted as "double," a female student attending a magnet school in Chicago explained it in this way:

In some ways it is easier for a female because you got two strikes. First, you're Black. That's strike number one. Then, you're a woman. That's strike number two. They have two facets of minorities right there.

That same sentiment was expressed by a student attending a magnet school in Washington, D.C.: "At first, to be a female, that's a minority; and then to be an African American female—that's like killing two birds with one stone."

While this perception may be true, it may be based on another reality. What these students perceive as "killing two birds with one stone" may actually be linked to societal and school perceptions of African American females as being in isolated, periphery service roles (Irvine, 1990, p. 75). That is, African American females are too far removed from the center of power to be a threat.

Concerning fear of African American males, a female student at a private school in Chicago best captured students' thoughts:

I think the world *period* is more intimidated by African American males than it is by African American females. I think that's a big part of the reason why there's that thought for African American females because I know I met a White man once and he was scared to death of the Black male I was with. But he [the Black male] did not find him intimidating at all. I just think that the world in general finds African American men more intimidating, more problematic, you know. They just have all these problems with them.

This perception is not without merit. Irvine (1990) reported, "Put simply, black males are probably the most feared, least likely to be identified with, and least likely to be effectively taught" (p. 78). It is the fear factor that can severely limit African American males' academic preparation and therefore lead to fewer choices following high school.

Influence of Athletics and Academics

A student attending an inner-city school in Chicago stated, "I think it's easier for some males because they play basketball and stuff and the colleges let them in with scholarships." At the same school, another student said, "It seems like females get more academic scholarships." Another student remarked, "Black males, they have to get in college through athletics, and females, they work their way up."

A female student attending a suburban school in Atlanta also spoke about the influence of athletics on the African American college choice process: "I think African American males have it easier because they are more looking for the sport athletics." Another student in that same discussion said, "I would say that the girls have the academics and the guys have the athletics."

Implicit in these students' discussions about the influences on African American students' choosing to participate in higher education is basically the financial resources available: How will schooling get paid? As a male student in Atlanta remarked with regard to sports, "That's where the money is." No doubt, it is for this reason that these students were so unanimous in identifying scholarships through athletics or academics as crucial to the college choice process.

Expectations of Society

Societal expectations are closely linked to what the students I interviewed perceived to be their sources of encouragement. That is, African American females are expected to be more academically talented; therefore, they are encouraged more to consider higher education. For example, a student attending a magnet school in Chicago stated, "They say that males can only do construction."

In a different way, a female student described how the desire to increase African American males' participation in higher education also demonstrates the lower expectations for them:

> Now, they are really striving for Black males to go to college. They usually strive for boys because they always think girls have a higher potential for learning and catch on quicker, but it was kind of racist in the class because the girls, they just expected them to get it.

The perceptions of these students indicate that African American females tend to perceive that their male peers are influenced primarily by the lure of athletics to go to college. On the other hand, African American males generally perceive that their female peers are more encouraged for their academics and are expected by society to go to college. While these views might be stereotypical, these findings could provide clues to the perceived barriers that African Americans, particularly males, experience in planning their postsecondary education.

When these perceptions are unpackaged, what is obvious is that the financial aspect of higher education is an important consideration. This finding is consistent with my previous research (Freeman, 1997). The African American students in this sample perceived that males are lured by athletics, which could have a negative effect on males who are not athletic. If a male has concentrated on athletics as an avenue to pay for his schooling, by the time he reaches tenth grade, he might realize that that option is unavailable; therefore, he would not have prepared himself for higher education. These findings also point to African American students' perceived views of the role that racism plays in students not choosing higher education. Underlying the idea of fear of African American male students and of females benefiting from fitting two special categories is the students' perception that males are not receiving adequate encouragement to continue their education beyond high school. These perceptions are supported by researchers such as Irvine (1990). In this sense, these findings show the very important role that people outside the home, particularly teachers and counselors, play in influencing African Americans to consider college attendance (Freeman, 1997). Bateman and Hossler (1996) write that "while teachers and counselors have been found to have little impact on the choice process for White students, they may be important to African American males" (p. 78). They also need role models other than athletes in the community.

As the findings in this chapter demonstrate, societal expectations are important in terms of individuals' perceptions of their options. Teachers play a particularly important role in transmitting expectations of African Americans, particularly males, and are influential in keeping African American males in schools.

Just as Bateman and Hossler (1996) found in their study, the influences on the college choice process of African Americans is a topic that bears much greater understanding. Especially for researchers and policymakers who wish to understand the predisposition of African American males and females to seek higher education, much more research needs to be conducted on gender differences.

CHAPTER 4

Economic Expectation and College Choice

Academicians continue to be in denial about students' economic expectation from higher education even though surveys such as the one completed by Boyer (1987) demonstrated that in the late 1980s an overwhelming number of college-bound high school students (90 percent) indicated that they were considering college as a means of getting a good job and that parents (88 percent) were equally concerned about the return on their investment, especially considering the high cost of attending higher education institutions today. Furthermore, the economics of education and college choice theorists have solidly documented that economic expectations influence students' college choice process (Anderson & Hearn, 1992; Hearn, 1991).

Given the linkage between economic expectation and college choice, one rationale for the fluctuation of African Americans' participation in higher education could be their perceptions of potential economic gain after higher education (Anderson & Hearn, 1992; Hossler, Braxton, & Coppersmith, 1989; Orfield et al., 1984). That is, when African Americans perceive they will receive a more favorable return on their investment in higher education, there will be an increase in the number of African Americans choosing to go to college. For example, according to Perlman (1973), following the euphoria of the 1960s, in the 1970s, when they perceived that after completing higher education African Americans did not receive employment commensurate with their level of schooling, many African Americans began to ask, "Will college make a difference?"

In what ways do the economic expectations of African American high school students influence their educational plans? What can be learned from the perceptions of these students as to their economic expectations that will be useful in explaining the fluctuation of their participation in higher education? Examining these questions can shed light on what Obgu (1978) defines as students' understanding of the limitations of their employment options.

College choice theorists and economics of education theorists (e.g., Becker, 1975; Cohn, 1979; Johns, Morphet, & Alexander, 1983; Thurow, 1972) have suggested that the expected cost of attendance and the future earning potential expected as a result of attending college are the two primary factors that students consider in their perception of the value of higher education, although economic status, race, and the education of their parents may have a bearing on future earning potential. Future earning potential has been greatly underexplored as it relates to whether African American students choose higher education.

In an ethnographic study, Ogbu (1978) describes how economic expectations might impact African American students' interest in schooling. He argues that members of a social group that faces a job ceiling recognize that they face it and that this knowledge shapes their children's academic behavior. Mickelson (1990) divides students' attitudes toward schooling into two categories: "abstract attitudes, embodying the Protestant ethic's promise of schooling as a vehicle for success and upward mobility, and concrete attitudes, reflecting the diverse empirical realities that people experience with respect to returns on education from the opportunity structure" (p. 45). According to Mickelson, students' realities vary according to their perceptions and understanding of how the significant adults in their lives receive more equitable or less equitable wages, jobs, and promotions relative to their educational credentials. According to this notion, students are influenced by the perceptions that shape their realities. Better understanding this idea can shed light on how African American students can aspire to go to college but can believe that actually doing so might not be economically viable. Since many African Americans hold jobs not commensurate with their level of schooling, even after higher education, this understandably influences students' perceptions of whether college would be a worthwhile investment. In a study of African American valedictorians and salutatorians, Arnold (1996) found that economic realities, along with other factors such as a bounded view of the world of work, shaped the outcome of the students in her sample. She reported that family structures, like economics, play a crucial, and often determining, role in the lives of African American and Latino valedictorians. Economic expectations are particularly a consideration for first-generation college-goers, as many African Americans were in Arnold's sample.

When African American students assess the labor market conditions of individuals like themselves who have completed a college degree, they often find individuals who are concentrated in professions below their level of schooling. As Wilson and Allen (1987) indicated, despite the higher educational attainment of the African American students in their sample, "a majority of these young adults were concentrated in either lower-level white collar jobs or blue collar jobs" (p. 69). Given this reality, it is not surprising then that African American high school students would be especially concerned about the return on their investment in higher education.

Students' Perceptions and Economic Expectations

The responses of the students interviewed indicate that they perceived economic expectations as a key influence on their choice to attend college or not. Their responses reflect that African Americans have a fear of either not having enough money to attend college or of not getting a job that pays commensurate with their level of education after completing college. The responses of these students clearly support what the literature indicates about the influence of economic expectations on college choice; that is, the statements made by African American students in this sample support the findings of economics of education and college choice theorists (e.g., Anderson & Hearn, 1992; Becker, 1975; Thurow, 1972), but their responses also add to the college choice literature by including, first, these students' perceptions of African Americans' primary value as being obtaining wealth or comfort rather than securing a specific occupation as pointed out in the study that Barnes (1992) conducted; and second, their recognition of job market limitations as suggested by the works of Ogbu (1978), Mickelson (1990), and Wilson and Allen (1987) (see figure 4. 1).

Figure 4.1. Economic Influences on College Choice

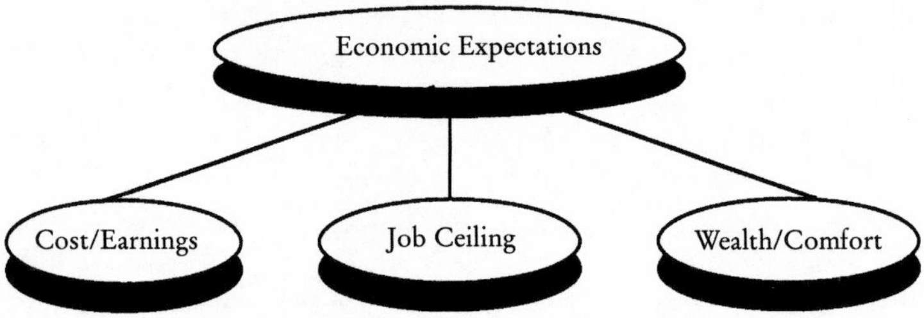

Expected Cost of College and Future Earnings

For African American students, the connection between what they perceive to be the cost of attending college and what they perceive as their future earning potential looms large in their consideration of higher education. The issue of lack of money to attend college was expressed by students across cities and school types. One student at a suburban school in Atlanta, Georgia, made a statement that was frequently repeated by students: "They don't have money to go." A student attending a private school in Chicago captured the essence of what students perceived about future earnings: "If you're not going to get better jobs, why go those four years for the same job?" At an independent school in New York, a student said:

> Well, maybe, because a lot of times when you are growing up, you might get the feeling and the outlook that, you know, it makes no sense because the jobs are not out there, and a lot of people feel that way—like, "Why am I going through all this when I'm not going to get a job, a job equivalent to what I would get if I didn't go; so what's the point?" I know a lot of people feel that way

According to researchers such as Thurow (1972), the perceptions of these high school students are solidly grounded, given that the value of higher education is impacted by economic status, race, and the education of their parents. That is, African Americans, particularly first-generation college-goers, are more likely over time, especially after the first five years of college, to receive a lower return on their investment than Whites (Freeman, 1997).

The students in this sample expressed that it was important for African American professionals to demonstrate to high school students that people like themselves had been successful in the job market after completing higher education. In response to the question of what could be done to help students gain a different perception of economic outcomes, a student at an independent school in New York said, "Just show people who are in colleges, I mean who have been to college, Black people preferably, who have jobs that make a lot of money, like maybe engineers and architects."

Although there is a great need to demonstrate to students that there are African Americans who have achieved and who can serve as role models, as supported by researchers such as Arnold (1996), who indicated the importance of role models on academic achievement, the fact of the matter, according to Wilson and Allen (1987), is that there are many African Americans concentrated in lower-level jobs even after completing college; they do not move on to these high-ranking positions.

Recognition of Job Market Ceilings Faced by Group Members

In keeping with what Ogbu (1978) suggested about students recognizing the job market ceiling faced by individuals of their own cultural group, these students clearly voiced their perceptions of the job market ceiling as an impediment to more African Americans choosing to go to college. For example, in an independent school in Chicago, a student responded, "People are unaware that there are opportunities out there after college. People just kind of see it as, you get out of college and then what do you do?" Another student attending school in New York asked, "Why should I go through four years or an extra four years of college to be a doctor or something like that for me to not get that job because of the color of my skin?"

Not only that, students have perceived, as Mickelson (1990) indicated, how individuals like themselves receive more equitable or less equitable job treatment relative to their educational credentials. A student attending a magnet school in Washington, D.C., had this to say:

> Of course, we have to be two times better than the Caucasian person and plus be more. In the case of being a male, you have to be three times better than the Caucasian person; you understand, as a female, we got to be four times as great, because they will test you to see if you know what you know. They say, "Well, you can't do this job." They say they think your aptitude is bad. So, it's difficult. It's very difficult.

The combination of perception of the job market limitations plus more or less equitable job treatment creates an insurmountable barrier in the minds of students considering whether or not to invest in higher education. At the same time, however, African American students are concerned about wealth and comfort.

Desire for Wealth or Comfort Rather than a Specific Occupation

While African American students admittedly are influenced about college choice by job market expectations, in keeping with what Barnes (1992) indicated in her study, the economic goals of these students are focused more on wealth or comfort than on a particular occupation. A student attending an inner-city school in New York, explaining why some African Americans decide to go to college, stated, "A better job. You want to increase your living standards and your position in society. You just don't want to be a high school graduate." Another student attending a private school in New York added this in reflecting on her decision to go to college when she was younger: "Wait, I want to go to college. And I was like, 'Ah, money.' So, I thought, 'I'll go to college and make money.'"

It has been this desire for wealth or comfort that has, perhaps, often caused researchers and educators to believe that African Americans are not serious about the college choice process. For example, it has been acknowledged that when the socioeconomic background has been held constant African Americans tend to have higher stated aspirations to participate in higher education than other groups (St. John, 1991). Yet they do not act on their aspirations as often as Whites. This could mean that their focus on wealth or comfort influences their stated aspirations. However, they may be hesitant to act on their aspirations given that, at the same time, they perceive that others like themselves face job market limitations in that there will be no way for them to achieve the wealth or comfort they desire.

In summary, African American students perceive that economic expectations play a significant role in their decision to attend college or not; they have generally voiced more interest in making money and bettering their position in society than in a particular occupation; they have concerns about the expected costs and the future earning potential; and they have recognized job market limitations.

The responses of these students clearly indicate that they perceive that when African Americans are making decisions about whether or not to attend college, an important consideration is, will it make a difference financially? When they look to other African Americans who have gone through the process, they often find individuals who are, according to Wilson and Allen (1987), concentrated in lower-level jobs. The perception of these limitations on economic opportunity could explain the fluctuations in the number of African American high school students who choose to pursue a college degree. Obviously, when students recognize limitations and cannot clearly see a return on that investment, they are much less likely to choose to invest in higher education. The question then becomes how to motivate and stimulate their desire to go to college when they perceive job market ceilings.

High schools, colleges, and universities could do more to help students understand the process of entering the job market after completing their college degrees, to encourage them to select a satisfying occupation, and to explore expectations after entering the market. College recruitment offices could do a much better job of helping potential college-goers, especially first-generation college-goers, to understand the linkages between college and transition to the labor market. It is clear that while college choice theorists have primarily focused on socioeconomic background, economic expectation is an area that requires more attention, from both research and practice aspects. Whether or not educators acknowledge it, when students consider postsecondary education, especially students who perceive labor market limitations, they will continue to ask, "Will college make a difference financially?"

Part Two
School Influences

CHAPTER 5

Curriculum Issues and Choice

The curriculum, even at the elementary and secondary school levels, has much to do with whether or not African American students choose higher education. Just as soul is an essential part of an individual, the curriculum can be defined as the soul—the central part—of a school at any level, whether primary, secondary, or postsecondary. A school's curriculum validates an individual's culture, history, and sense of self, that is, what is possible. Therefore, when culture, in this case African American culture, is not included in the very heart of the school curriculum, the feeling that something is missing is created within those students. Banks (1988) said it best when he wrote, "It is important for students to experience a curriculum that not only presents the experience of ethnic and cultural groups in accurate and sensitive ways, but that also enables them to see the experiences of both mainstream and minority groups from the perspectives of different cultural, racial, and ethnic groups" (p. 161).

An absence of an education about people like themselves in the heart of the school curriculum could diminish students' desire to learn, which will obviously influence whether those students decide to persist beyond secondary school. However, researchers have not explored the role that the curriculum, particularly the noninclusion of group culture in the curriculum at the elementary

51

and secondary school levels, plays in impacting students' decision to attend college or not.

This chapter primarily examines the following: (1) the influence on the decision making of these students about higher education participation by the inclusion or absence of their culture in the curriculum at both the secondary and college levels, and (2) African American students' perceptions of the influence of the curriculum in secondary school on their college choice process. As previously indicated, because many African American students are first-generation college-goers, they look to the school for guidance. It is ironic, then, that the very system they look to often fails them, particularly in the area of curriculum. Building on Mickelson's (1990) notion that individuals' realities are based on the experiences of people like themselves, the absence of validation of culture, in this case African American culture, in the curriculum surely influences decision making about the possibility of actual higher education participation. This would be consistent with Ogbu's (1978) findings that members of a social group recognize the limitations that their group members face and that this information shapes their academic behavior.

The Influence of Curriculum on African Americans and College Choice

It is absolutely astonishing that college choice theorists have not considered the role of a culturally relevant curriculum and its influence on African American students' postsecondary educational planning. It is as though the fact that many African American students have underachieved, which impacts their higher education plans, is completely divorced from the curriculum. Although the influence of a culturally relevant curriculum on college choice has not been explored, linkages have clearly been established between the curriculum and its effect on African American students' achievement (Hollins, 1996; King, 1995). Since college choice theorists have documented the influence of academic achievement on students choosing higher education (Hossler & Gallagher, 1987; Bateman & Hossler, 1996), it is not difficult to infer the influence of curriculum on students' achievement and thus on their higher education plans. As Hollins (1996) indicated, for African American children, the "discontinuity between the home-culture and school learning ultimately disrupts the learning process for many children and the resulting failure may lead them to reject the Euro-American culture and school learning as well" (p. 84).

The school curriculum, as defined by Hollins (1996), is "in fact that package of knowledge, skills, and perspectives that prepares us to develop the attributes of thought and behavior that comply with the prescribed norms" (p. 82). Inconsistences in compliance with these norms by different cultural groups, in this case African Americans, can lead to various group members questioning their identity, being turned off to learning, or underperforming academically. In what ways does the curriculum influence the choice process?

Typically, college choice theorists have focused on the tracking of students (that is, placement in general, college preparatory, or vocational programs) and the selection of courses that influence their college choice, not how aspects of the curriculum have impacted African American students' motivation and aspiration to go to college. For example, a study by Pelavin and Kane (1990) focused on the selection of courses and its influence on students' college choice. However, there are other aspects of the elementary and secondary curricula that have implications for African American students choosing whether or not to continue their studies. Drawing on the works of Banks (1988), Hollins (1996), King (1995), and Ladson-Billings (1994), a relationship between the curriculum of the school attended and the motivation and aspiration of African American students to participate in higher education can be inferred.

According to these theorists, the lack of a culturally relevant or culturally centered knowledge curriculum (King, 1995; Ladson-Billings, 1994), the exclusion of cultural history from the curriculum or a balanced historical perspective (Banks, 1988; Hollins, 1996), and the curriculum as contested terrain (Hollins, 1996; King, 1995; Swartz, 1996) can impact students' academic achievement and thereby influence their postsecondary plans. For example, as Ladson-Billings (1994) notes, "Culturally relevant teaching is about questioning (and preparing students to question) the structural inequality, the racism, and the injustice that exist in society" (p. 128). More directly, King (1995) states, "Euro-American cultural knowledge that is represented and valorized in school curricula is culture-centered with respect to its referent, the existing U.S. social framework, not because it is Eurocentric, but because it serves to legitimate the dominant White middle-class normative cultural model" (p. 270). Presenting the culture of African Americans according to a White normative model can cause students to question their own identity and self-worth. This questioning can not only harm their sense of self but also result in a belief that their life choices may be limited, particularly their choices beyond secondary school.

There is no question that the curriculum is contested terrain because the heart and soul of how students' knowledge about themselves and others is constructed is based on what they learn in the school setting. King (1995) states it in this way: "Close consideration of the contestation over the curriculum reveals a recurring pattern of cultural negation/assimilation versus cultural affirmation/revitalization within a historical dialectic of ideological conflict and cultural hegemony" (p. 266). Therefore, given the importance of the curriculum on students' academic achievement, it is quite surprising that college choice theorists have not investigated the influence of the curriculum on their postsecondary educational plans.

Students' Perceptions of the Influence of Curriculum on College Choice

The perceptions of the students in my study about the curriculum and its influence on choice can be divided into three categories: (1) missing history, (2) absence of validation, and (3) concrete realities (see figure 5. 1).

Missing History

Students at three independent schools were asked how they felt about the lack of instruction in African American history at their schools. A New York student replied, "There should be Black history." Another New York student said, "They don't really teach you about Black history. Like this is Black history month; we'll focus on Black people. But it's not worked into the curriculum...as a whole thing." A Chicago student said, "I know early world history, and they don't incorporate African Americans in their history."

Figure 5.1. African American High School Students' Perceptions of the Influence of Curriculum on College Choice

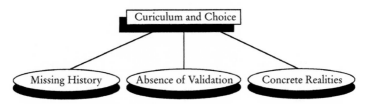

These statements reflect the sentiments of Banks (1988) that African American history is usually relegated to special holidays such as Black History Month and is largely invisible in the curriculum during the rest of the year. Banks also makes the point that most educators believe that African American history, even when included, is only necessary for other African American students or to help reduce ethnic conflict at schools that have racial conflict. However, it is interesting to note that even many African American students do not believe they know their own history. As one student from an independent school in Chicago remarked:

> I've had a hard time in African American history because I don't know about Black history because I was never taught. I was always taught other things. It's so backwards. I think it's crazy. How do you skip the years which were some of the most important times, which helped in the creation of America? How do you skip that—from early to modern?

The whole notion of omitting the culture of different groups from the school's curriculum is described by Swartz (1996) as essentially being sociopolitical and power driven. She says that the debate over the centrality of race, class, and gender groups in the curriculum is not about the relative importance of historical figures and events; nor is it about the impact of the curricular experience on self-esteem or the modeling of race, gender, and class heroes and heroines. According to her, "It is a debate over emancipatory versus hegemonic scholarship and the maintenance or disruption of the Eurocentrically bound 'master script' that public schools currently impart to their students" (p. 164). As such, unless perspectives can be disempowered through misrepresentation, they are altogether omitted from the "master script." It is the omission of individuals' culture from the master script, especially history courses, that makes them feel as though they have no cultural relevance. Cultural relevance allows African American students to maximize their academic potential (Ladson-Billings, 1994), which enables them to believe that higher education is an option.

Absence of Validation

Not having one's culture validated in the curriculum can cause students to question the importance of who they are, as one student from an independent school in New York asks when he questions whether European history creates the ideal school: "I think when they are young, you need to teach them the background of other cultures. Not only European. European history, then are you saying [it's] the ideal for school or something like that?" Other students indicated that equal to the absence of African Americans in the curriculum are compounding subtleties which invalidate their culture, and as one independent school student from Los Angeles stated, "You do after a time notice that sometimes you're not treated the same. When you're with a group of White people, you're not treated the same as they are. It's very implicit; it's not like, 'We don't want you around.'" Another student from an independent school in New York put it this way: "There are teachers in this school that have been hostile about science and evolution, like, 'I had nothing to do with those Black people.'"

The negative effects of the lack of culture validation are brought about, according to Ladson-Billings (1994), by African American students not seeing their history, culture, or background represented in the textbooks or curriculum or by seeing their history, culture, or background distorted by staffing patterns at schools (most African Americans are in low-level positions) and by the tracking of African American students into the lowest-level classes. Such lack of validation of ethnic groups in the curriculum silences groups, robs them of voice and perspective, and marginalizes and disconnects individuals in their time and place (Swartz, 1996).

When individuals are not validated in the curriculum, they also come to recognize their academic limitations (Ogbu, 1978). In other words, from a college choice perspective, when students realize the disconnection between their desire to achieve and the limitations faced by individuals like themselves, choosing college participation becomes a dilemma—the abstract possibilities transform into concrete realities.

Concrete Realities

As described in chapter 4, students' aspirations are shaped by their perception of the concrete, racially based realities that may limit their futures. Ogbu (1978) stated, for example, that because of the low job ceiling that Aftican Americans have experienced, they have perceived that they are unable to improve their economic and social conditions even after being educated. Abstract attitudes and concrete realities are shaped and reinforced by the way the students are presented or excluded from the curriculum. The following statement from a student attending a school in New York clearly indicates the perception of students that African Americans need concrete examples that higher education is economically viable:

> You have to show them Black people can achieve and, you know, you have to lay a foundation.... My teacher would be like, "All right, everybody was White except for Nefertiti because she was too Black to say she's White." I think what you need to do is lay down the foundation for the culture, and I think you also have to present careers for them.

From these perspectives, not having African American culture in the curriculum—particularly not including African American history, not validating their culture, or not demonstrating the possibilities—can impact the decision of these students to attend college or not. One student at an independent school in Chicago summed up the issue of college choice and curriculum when he said the following:

> The true reasons for [African Americans] not attending higher education, even if you go through high school: One is economic—the money not being there. Two has to do with race relations in the country and their view on other people.

While the influence of the curriculum on higher education participation choice has not been explored, this chapter demonstrates that there are linkages between students' perceptions of their culture being excluded from the curriculum at all levels of schooling and their sense of self. Just as research has demonstrated that there is a clear relationship between excluding students' culture from the curriculum and academic achievement (Banks, 1988; Ladson-Billings, 1994; Mickelson, 1990; Ogbu, 1978), it is not difficult to conclude that if students are not achieving academically at the primary and secondary levels, the option of choosing college will be greatly diminished. It is noteworthy that not only did African American students perceive the connection between the curriculum and college choice, they viewed it from the perspective of what is missing from the curriculum. That is, these students spoke passionately about their culture, particularly their history, not being represented in the curriculum, and they also expressed in their own words what it felt like not to be validated in the school setting.

The African American students in this study expressed concern that their culture is not appreciated and therefore not seriously included in the school curriculum. From these students' perspective, the absence of their culture from the curriculum is one of the barriers African Americans face in choosing higher education participation. According to these students, including African American culture in the curriculum would, at a minimum, improve their sense of self and instill in them a passion for learning. Given these realities, it is understandable that these students would echo the importance of emphasizing cultural awareness in the curriculum. This aspect of their perceptions is one that college choice and economics of education theorists should explore in much greater detail. As pointed out in this chapter and suggested by Mickelson (1990) and Ogbu (1978), when the souls of individuals are missing in the essential part of the school curriculum, the academic behavior of these individuals is affected, thereby limiting their choices beyond high school.

CHAPTER 6

Channeling Long and Wrong

How the seeds of desire for upward mobility are planted, who plants them, and how they are cultivated are interesting phenomena. Equally interesting is what happens when there are strong desires, and yet no cultivation of those desires. This metaphor of the seeds of desire describes what often happens when students, in this case African Americans, have the desire for upward mobility through education but lack the forces to cultivate their desires into the actuality of college participation—which is especially the case for first-generation college-goers. While there is research on how the seeds get planted, that is, influences on the college choice process (e.g., Hearn, 1991; Hossler & Gallagher, 1987), researchers and educators are often perplexed when it comes to determining a prescription for cultivating the seeds (mediating the decision-making process) when there are social or cultural differences.

There is widespread agreement among researchers that the process of deciding to attend college is begun in the home by the parents and, more often than not, is determined by the father's level of education and occupation (Anderson & Hearn, 1992; Hossler, Braxton, & Coopersmith, 1989). As part 1 of this book suggests, the influences on African American students can include extended family members, and equally as important as the father's level of education is the influence of the mother. There is a lot less known about what, if anything, outside the home can influence the desire. However, some researchers have examined the forces outside the home which channel the decision-making process from several perspectives, including geographical and school factors (Orfield et al., 1984; Thomas, 1980).

By all accounts, for students who come from homes where parents are not college educated, the role of schools in helping these students fill the information void about the college choice process takes on greater proportions. The issue, then, becomes whether schools can or should act as channelers in the college choice process of students who are socially or culturally different.

The intent of this chapter is to explore several questions as they relate to channeling: (1) What exactly is channeling? (2) How does channeling impact students' decision process to choose to participate in higher education? (3) Can forces such as school factors mediate social and cultural differences, for example, African American students' choosing to pursue postsecondary education?

Understanding Channeling

The term *channeling* can be defined as the environmental forces (whether individuals, institutions, or circumstances) that influence the direction of students' postsecondary choices. By all accounts, the influences on students are both individual and familial and school-related factors. The question as to the degree of influence of either individual or school factors on different cultural groups such as African Americans has been greatly underexplored.

Orfield et al. (1984) conducted a comprehensive study of access to and choice concerning higher education in Chicago which concluded that minorities are channeled into college based on defined geographic locations where they live. Channeling, as it relates to college choice, of course, cuts across both social and cultural capital and economic and financial capital. That is, the more capital an individual has, whether cultural or economic, the more likely it will be for that individual to be influenced by forces internal to the home. Chapters 1 and 4 illustrate channeling influences internal to the home (see figure 6. 1).

Figure 6.1. Channeling Influences on College Choice Internal to the Home

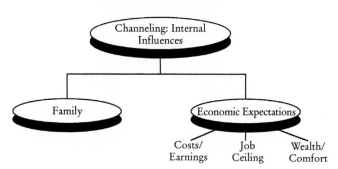

Channeling: Internal Influences

Channeling internal to the home, as pointed out in chapter 1, includes the influences of the family on the postsecondary decision-making process of their children. Understanding channeling helps to provide information on not just who in the family influences the decision process but also the ways in which family influences this process. In addition to family members, economics also plays a role in channeling students to choose higher education.

As demonstrated in chapter 4, individuals who are not a part of the majority population are channeled by economic expectations of costs and expected earnings after college. In this instance, African American students can be influenced negatively by job market ceilings faced by other African Americans. While family is an example of individuals influencing the decision-making process, economic expectations are an example of circumstances that channel the direction students will go in. And, since many African Americans are first-generation college-goers and legitimately perceive the job market limitations faced by other African Americans, they often turn to external forces to influence their decision regarding higher education.

Channeling: External Influences

Outside the home, high school location (rural, urban, or suburban), teachers, and counselors have tremendous influence on channeling students to choose or not to choose college participation (Orfield et al., 1984; Morrison, 1989; Barnes, 1992) (see figure 6.2). According to Barnes (1992), "47. 5% of the African American twelfth grade males staying in her study reported that assignment to excellent teachers helped keep them in school" (p. 106). She writes further, "It seems clear that one way to hold African-American males' attention and keep them interested in their school work is to assign them the best teachers in school. These teachers will hold their interest, educate them, and help them graduate" (p. 106).

Figure 6.2. Channeling Influences on College Choice External to the Home

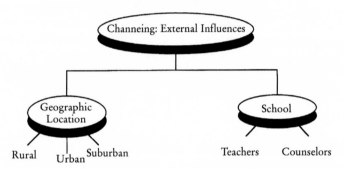

Counselors play an equally important function. For example, as Morrison (1989) writes, "An opportunity for minority students and their parents to engage in programs that provide current institutional information, a visual campus overview, interaction with faculty and alumni, and questions and answers can be of considerable benefit" (pp. 13–14). It is typically counselors who help facilitate this process for high school students.

One of the most recent studies that specifically investigates the choice process of underrepresented groups and looks at the environmental influences outside the home channeling student choice is the work of Levine and Nidiffer (1996). In their book *Beating the Odds: How the Poor Get to College,* they interviewed twenty-four students from impoverished conditions, including African American students. They found a common theme from all of their subjects regarding "how they came to attend college" (p. 65). This common element "put simply was an individual who touched or changed the students' lives" (p. 65).

The quality of the high school attended (see figure 6.2) understandably also has implications for whether students are channeled into choosing college participation (Alexander, D'Amico, Fennessey, & McDill, 1978; Anderson & Hearn, 1992; Boyle, 1966). For example, students at the top of their class in an urban school are less likely than their counterparts in a suburban school to have had access to college recruiters and to have visited a college campus, and are more likely to have missed even the basic information necessary to participate in the higher education process. Students who attend private or independent schools and suburban schools are more likely to be influenced, in fact have already been channeled, to attend college than students who attend inner-city high schools. More than the schools themselves, it is the services provided by those schools, for example, teachers and counselors: "Schools in affluent suburbs encourage college attendance and channel their students into college preparatory curricula; schools in poor or working class neighborhoods tend to prepare students for jobs not requiring college training" (Jencks, as cited in Orfield et al., 1984, p. 28). As Orfield et al. (1984) explain in terms of channeling, changes in the school situation can change outcomes (p. 28). However, it is safe to say that schools have channeled African Americans for too long in the wrong direction.

External Influences: Students' Perceptions

In my study, beyond family influences, students' perceptions of the value of higher education generally were most influenced by teachers and counselors and less by the geographic location of their school. Students typically perceived that a college degree or lack thereof would impact their position in life.

More Interested Teachers

The students interviewed placed greater emphasis on the value of having teachers who instill a passion in students, who believe in the ability of African American students to learn, and who push students to maximize their potential. Voicing his opinion about the role of teachers in motivating students to go to college, a student at a magnet school in Los Angeles had this to say:

> I've been fortunate enough to have a teacher who [has] made me work for everything. Mr. Sweeney is a real mathematics teacher. Some other mathematics teacher might not be as good, but what I learned was college math analysis, and that's because Mr. Sweeney got out his paycheck and went and bought these college prep books.

"[Schools also need to] have a lot of Black teachers," said an independent school student in New York. The following insight came from an inner-city New York student:

> [There needs to be] a different type of teaching program. Like [now] most students are in the chairs and teachers are at the board. I think more discussions should be involved in the classrooms and not so much reading the books.

Related to the need for good teachers, another New York student said, "Enthusiastic teachers...come across interesting....Teachers are everything." With respect to African American teachers, a student from Chicago said, "There are not that many Black teachers here at all; and I mean this school is an excellent school for an education, but it would probably even be better."

Another student stated:

> I think it's school. I don't have many friends outside of school, but the couple that I do have, the way they describe their school, it's like the teachers don't even care if they come to school every day...; and I don't know if it's exaggerated, but it is completely different from here.

Another inner-city student from Washington, D.C., rated teachers as highly as friends by stating, "Teachers and friends... encourage them to go on with their education." A student from Los Angeles elaborated on the influence of teachers:

> You know, I had teachers who...were strong. They motivated you to do your work and helped you a lot. I think some schools in the Black community...don't have enough money to buy books that will teach the kids so, you know, the teachers don't want to teach it. Then it's not good material, and the students don't want to learn. So, I think...you [have] to get your money

together, put it in the schools where it counts, . . . and help these students.

Actively Involved Counselors

Observations and conversations with school officials confirmed statements made by the students about the importance of having counselors actively involved in the process to increase the number of students applying to college. I personally noted that in those schools that had structured counseling programs, there tended to be a greater number of students interested in going on to college. As would be expected, the private schools had active college-related events. However, in those public schools that had active counseling programs, their success in stimulating and preparing students for participation in higher education seemed equal to private schools. The following statements demonstrate how strongly students felt about active counselor involvement in assisting students in the college process.

A student from a Los Angeles magnet school said, "Because we're pushed. We're pushed to go on to higher education and then get a job. That's Ms. Getter's whole basis for being here basically." An inner-city student from New York said, "Maybe get some college programs in high school to prepare them for college so they won't go and be scared what it's going to be. Counselors generally have the information as far as scholarships." A Washington, D.C., magnet school student added:

> Certain counselors have information about internships, different opportunities so that you can get to work for us, specific jobs where you get to go into that field of your interest to see if that's what you really want to do. If you keep in contact with these [counselors] then, I mean, these who haven't really had the opportunity.

"I've got Career Beginnings. . . . It's a program to help me decide what college I want to go to and where . . . and helps you with your financial aid," added an inner-city student in New York.

A suburban school student in Atlanta, Georgia, said, "They let us know about upcoming scholarships from this point on. They have something like a senior letter and every time a new scholarship comes up they put it on that list." In Chicago, an independent school student said, "Junior year you start having classes about college courses. You have to have like required meetings with the counselor."

As to what he thought was important, an inner-city school student in Washington, D.C., stated, "Counseling." However, some students do not see counselors as a positive influence. A student from an independent school in New York found that "counselors don't help. They discourage you, especially in public schools. They tell you such things as you're not qualified. They don't care."

Researchers need to look at the schools whose teachers and counselors are not doing their jobs to motivate as well as educate students, which includes encouraging them to participate in higher education, for primary and secondary schooling only lay a foundation to build upon.

The African American students who participated in this study indicated that school factors play a major role in shaping their interest in college. There is every reason to take them seriously. These findings, then, support the suggestion of Orfield et al. (1984) that channeling, when used effectively, can mediate social and cultural differences, can impact the financial aid process and students' economic outlook, and can influence the type of postsecondary school selected and subsequent college experiences. These conclusions in no way mitigate findings from previous studies or researchers (e.g., Hearn, 1991; Levine & Nidiffer, 1996; Stage & Hossler, 1989) who suggest the importance of individual and familial influences on the college choice process.

What seems evident is that individuals who are first-generation college-goers or who have different social and culture capital tend to perceive that the school can and should provide them the necessary guidance to steer them toward college. In other words, given the fact that these students only listed forces within the school as influences on their college choice process, school factors can have, at least in the opinions of these students, a great deal of influence in channeling the direction of their choice.

As indicated by these students, it has become increasingly clear that the information pipeline to students, particularly to those students who are not the recipients of the intergenerational benefit of having higher education passed down to them, must begin much earlier, and it must be incorporated in some structured format within the schools. It is in this way, as Orfield et al. (1984) suggested, that channeling can improve the choice process for students. This does not mean that the information process has to be a specific course imposed on teachers, in response to those who feel that public schools cannot be all things to all people or are already doing enough. However, it is noteworthy that among the schools that participated in this study, those public schools that had structured counseling programs (all independent schools had them) had a larger number of students going on to college.

It is clear that current models are not working, and these students' ideas are solid ones. It would be difficult to find anyone who would disagree that better teachers and interested counselors are needed and that instilling possibilities earlier is indicated.

These research findings do not disagree with student choice theorists' findings that indicate the importance of parental education and income. However, when these students describe possible solutions to African Americans participating in higher education, they point out the importance of the school. Understanding this in the context of the African American culture has merit. The school system plays an even greater role when parents themselves have no postsecondary education, as many African American students are still first-generation college-goers.

An important conclusion of this chapter is that there are forces that can cultivate the seeds of desire for upward mobility (that is, a desire to pursue postsecondary studies). Better understanding how factors within the elementary and secondary schools can channel students who are culturally and socially different into choosing higher education is a challenge that K–12 and higher educators can jointly address.

CHAPTER 7

Decision Making by High School Type: High Schools Successful in Channeling

Although much has been written about the influence of the location of the high school attended on a student's decision to attend college (Boyle, 1966), it is not so much the location of the high school as the funding available and services provided that can make the difference in the ability of schools to channel students toward higher education.

To imply that simply because a high school is located in the inner-city the students attending that school will not desire to attend college does not hold true, as demonstrated in the cross section of students in my study from the different high school types who indicated their desire to continue their studies after high school. While it is recognized that not as many students attending inner-city high schools actually go to college as those from magnet or suburban high schools, there are many students attending inner-city schools who desire to pursue higher education and, depending on the type of college-geared services provided by the high school, will act on that desire. It is for this reason that it is extremely important to examine various high school types to determine what it is that makes some successful in influencing students to apply to college, rather than to write off certain high schools because of their location.

This chapter, therefore, will focus on those aspects of various high school types that have been successful in channeling students to elect college and will look specifically at (1) the characteristics of the high schools that assist students in the college choice process and (2) how these high schools differ from the high schools that are not as successful in channeling students.

High School Types and Students' Choice: What the Research Indicates

Boyle's (1966) seminal work titled "The Effect of the High School on Students' Aspirations" provides the best framework for understanding how students at various high school types differ in choosing higher education participation. In reviewing the works of other researchers, such as Coleman, as a way to summarize his findings, Boyle proposed, as set forth in figure 7.1, a network of interrelated factors to explain the pattern of influence of high schools on students. He indicated that individual factors, such as scholastic ability and motivation, are influenced by each high school's (1) basic factors (structural characteristics and population composition), (2) "society-level" consequences of the basic factors (the divergence of the structural characteristics and peer groups of the high school), and (3) individual-level consequences (scholastic ability and motivation). More specifically, regarding the divergent educational standards and scholastic development of the high school, Boyle, citing Wilson, explained that some schools provide their students with better educational opportunities than others due to residential segregation. As an example, he wrote that "teachers in predominately working-class schools came to expect less of their students than teachers in more middle-class schools and to key their teaching to these expectations" (p. 631).

After his review of previous studies and findings from his own study, Boyle drew three important conclusions:

1. The population composition of a high school does have an important effect on the aspirations of its students, but the effect is much stronger in larger cities than smaller communities.

2. One important but (at least in metropolitan areas) partial explanation for this effect is the differential success of high schools in the scholastic abilities of their students.

Figure 7.1. Schematic Diagram of Factors Leading to Variation in the College Aspirations of Students Attending Different High Schools

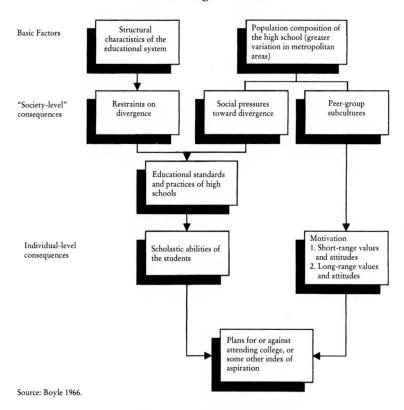

Source: Boyle 1966.

3. The failure of scholastic ability to explain all of the effects of metropolitan high schools points to the existence of other explanations, such as the influence of the peer group, but occupational or social-class values do not sufficiently account for these effects (p. 639).

Essentially, Boyle suggested that the high school attended does explain some difference in students' postsecondary education plans, but that there is a great deal left unexplained as it relates to the effect of the high school on students' aspirations.

Regarding students' scholastic aptitude, more recent studies have focused on the influence of course selection on students' decision to attend college. For example, Pelavin and Kane (1990) reported that students who were enrolled in algebra and geometry, at least one year of a laboratory science, and at least two years of a foreign language were more likely to choose college. Of these courses, they concluded that taking two years of a foreign language was the greatest predictor, followed by one year of geometry and one year of laboratory sciences. They compiled data that demonstrated that approximately 40 percent of White students took geometry as opposed to only 19 percent of African Americans.

The question that continues to go unanswered in Boyle's and Pelavin and Kane's research is, why is it that African American students aspire in much greater numbers than White students to attend college and yet in the end do not act on their aspirations? The assumed cause is either lack of motivation on the part of the students or simply the location of the high school attended. However, as Boyle noted, teacher expectations play a major role in students' aspirations becoming reality. In support of this notion, as previously stated, Hearn et al. (1995) indicated that there is a disjunction between African American students' expectations and their attainment. If teachers expect students to fail, then it is unlikely that they will enroll in college preparatory classes, participate in extracurricular activities, or have the necessary information to prepare for higher education. Although previous research has focused on the effect of the high school on students' college aspirations, the focus of the research has been on the individual as opposed to examining characteristics of high schools, regardless of location, that have been successful in motivating their students to choose higher education.

Characteristics of High Schools Successful in Channeling Students toward College

Taking a lesson from private and independent schools, magnet schools, and other public schools that tend to have a higher number of students who choose higher education, one common characteristic that these schools share is a structured counseling program. They do not merely have counselors; they have guidance and counseling programs that are targeted, purposeful, and meaningful. These schools also tend to (1) have linkages with higher education institutions to ease students' transition from high school to college, (2) have and demonstrate high expectations of their students, and (3) understand the importance of and use mentoring (see figure 7.2).

Figure 7.2. Characteristics of High Schools Successful in Channeling Students into Higher Education

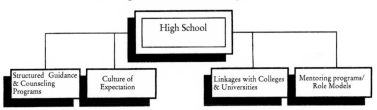

Structured Guidance and Counseling Programs

Although it is assumed that the parents of students who attend private and independent schools would be in the best position to assist their children, it is these schools that tend to have the most structured programs. Ironically, the use of guidance counselors tends to work inversely. That is, the schools that need the services the most tend to have the least amount of counseling, whereas the programs that have a higher concentration of parents who would have more information available to them tend to offer more counseling.

The more successful counseling programs provide an array of services. However, the feature that seemed to stick out the most in the minds of the students surveyed in this study is the organized manner of the services. That is, beginning in tenth grade, students at private and independent schools are required to meet with a counselor. Recognizing that counselors are overloaded in most high school types, the counselors in the successful programs still require students to meet with them if for no other reason than to assess where students are in their planning process.

Given that some African American students have indicated that they are their own motivator and some are first-generation college applicants, these students freely discussed the guidance and direction that assisted them in considering and searching the higher education prospects available. For example, a student attending a magnet school in Chicago said, "I wanted to go to college so I started coming to the college career center, and I did get a lot of help from Mr. Smith and my counselors who were around me at the time."

It should not be assumed that inner-city high schools do not have any counseling programs. Some, in fact, do. For example, at an inner-city school in Chicago, students discussed a program they called "Career Beginnings." One of the students described it in this way: "It's a program to help me decide what college I want to go to and where." Admittedly, the students who participated in this program were selected, but, unfortunately, not until their senior year. Although this program began late, contrasted with an inner-city school where students are not receiving any services, it's better late than never. For example, a student said, "Basically at [this school] there is really no career counselor here for us to really talk to." At another inner-city school in New York, a student in the group that received no services (the non–college-bound students) indicated that the students felt that they had no help in the college process— that no one believed in them.

Although helping students understand the process is the first step, the more specific steps students need help with are the application process and the search for financial aid. As several students indicated, students do not consider higher education participation because they do not think they can afford it. The successful counseling programs help students address these issues.

As described in chapter 6, guidance counselors also provide students with invaluable help with finding sources of financial aid to allow them to attend college.

Culture of Expectations: Belief in Students' Abilities

Even though structured guidance and counseling programs are enormously important, without having created a culture of belief in the abilities of its students, a high school cannot be successful in motivating them to choose higher education. As Boyle (1966) indicated, within highly segregated high schools, particularly in urban areas, teachers key their expectations to the population that they serve. In support of this finding, Cuyjet (1997) suggested lowered expectations of peers and significant adults toward academic achievement as one explanation of why so many "Black men do not make it to college" (p. 6). However, Hearn, Griswold, Marine, and McFarland (1995) found that the aspirations of students in a segregated high school to participate in higher education actually increased; that is, being in an environment where students had similar culture and experiences actually motivated students.

Something almost magical occurs when teachers demonstrate their belief in the abilities of their students. As demonstrated in the previous chapter, particularly when that belief is demonstrated early (in elementary school), students develop the necessary inner strength to be able to overcome many obstacles. However, in my observation of these high schools, a characteristic of the successful schools is that they go beyond teacher expectations. These schools seem to have created a culture where the team of principal, teachers, and guidance counselors believe in the potential of their students. As an example, the principal at a suburban school in Atlanta openly discussed how he believed in the school's students and that he only wanted teachers and counselors who shared that philosophy. Although a suburban school, this school was predominately African American and had a high concentration of students who were from single-parent homes. There are examples of inner-city schools where principals hold similar beliefs. For example, a principal at an inner-city school in Washington, D.C., indicated that regardless of the conditions of his school he believed that it was important for the school to do the best for its students. He was clearly actively involved in every aspect of the operation of his school.

Conversely, it was easy to identify the schools that displayed the characteristic of disbelief in their students. These were the schools where the principals, teachers, and counselors openly first discussed the backgrounds of their students, their parental background, and the neighborhood—that is, the students are from single-parent homes and the neighborhood is filled with drug addicts. While we must not underestimate the influence of these characteristics on students' aspirations, it is also true that there are schools in similar settings that have established the characteristic of belief. These are the schools where structured programming is operationalized.

There has been widespread evidence of the importance of teacher expectations in relation to students' ability to achieve. For example, Foster (1997), Irvine (1990), and Ladson-Billings (1996) have written extensively about the influence of African American teachers on students' ability to learn. However, this has been underexamined in the college choice area and a great deal more research is needed to better understand how a culture of belief in students' abilities influences students to choose higher education.

Linkages with Colleges and Universities

To help instill a desire to participate in higher education in some students and to ease the transition of other students to higher education, the successful high schools also have established linkages with colleges and universities. These programs take on a number of dimensions, including having university speakers visit high schools and taking students on visits to college and university campuses. Obviously, these linkages are extremely important, particularly for students who have had no previous contact with colleges. Several students discussed how these linkages impacted them and their desire to continue their studies. For example, at a magnet school in Washington, D.C., a student was taking a course at Georgetown University. He described his experience in this way:

> I'm taking a course at Georgetown, so we get to experience a little of what it's like to be in a college atmosphere. . . . The whole experience is good because you get to see what you have to look forward to when you get into college—when it really starts to count.

Although other students did not indicate that they were taking courses on a college campus during the school year, several indicated that they had either attended conferences, participated in summer programs, or visited a college campus. A student attending a magnet school in Los Angeles stated, "I went to UCLA on a student leadership conference, and we [got] together [and discussed] ideas on how to be a leader and [chose] characteristics of a person we would make [a leader]."

Several of the high school programs had planned trips for students to visit college campuses. An inner-city school in Chicago, for example, plans several campus visits for its students each year. One student attending this particular school indicated that the school sent students to Morehouse College in Atlanta as well as other schools in Alabama. They were planning another trip in the spring to visit the University of Chicago and Southern Illinois University. Such interactions with college campuses, that many college-educated parents take for granted, are enormously important for these students. As one student attending a magnet school in Washington, D.C., indicated, getting prepared for college is a mind-set: "You have to get yourself prepared as well as your grades and as well as how you feel about yourself—your self-esteem."

Having the opportunity to interact with the college environment goes a long way with not only assisting students in developing the mind-set as they prepare for college, but also in developing survival strategies for after they enter college. The high schools that are successful in preparing students to consider higher education as an option understand the importance of incorporating these activities into their school program and college planning. These schools also understand the value of mentoring or providing role models for students.

Mentoring Programs and Role Models

While no formalized mentoring programs were directly observed at these high schools, several students indicated that they believed that African Americans who have achieved should be much more involved in mentoring students or, at a minimum, being a role model for students. These students' perceptions are supported by Cuyjet (1997), who discusses the absence of role models for African American men, particularly as a deterrent to their participation in higher education, as well as their being underprepared once they get to college.

In addition to arranging linkages with higher education institutions, the high schools that were successful in instilling a passion for higher education in their students also tended to arrange to have students interact with role models by bringing in successful people such as alumni to speak, or in some cases, the teachers themselves acted as role models through sharing their own college experiences with students.

However these schools have incorporated mentoring and role modeling into their programs, it is a very valuable service. One student attending a magnet school in Los Angeles indicated that students "need people who they can look up to." Despite the fact that a characteristic of the successful high schools is that they understand the value of providing mentoring models, even these programs do not incorporate mentoring into their program to the degree that they could. From the students' perspectives, there is a much greater need to do so. To summarize, a student at a magnet school in Chicago said it best: "Nowadays we have children who need counseling, and they need a pat on the back to tell them that what they're doing is good."

Mentoring is one way that students can receive both a pat on the back and the necessary guidance to better understand the process of preparing for college.

High Schools and Students' Aspirations: The Need for Greater Explication

While Boyle's (1966) model goes a long way in explaining the effect of high school on students' aspirations, there is a desperate need to expand on his model. Although he outlines the components that explain how high schools affect students' aspirations, his model appears to place most of the attention on students' background characteristics: where students come from (their neighborhoods), their socioeconomic status, and their peer groups. He discusses minimally the role of teacher expectations. However, as demonstrated in this chapter, greater emphasis needs to be placed not on what high schools do not do, but on what they can do to more positively affect students' desire to participate in higher education.

The characteristics noted here should be taken as just the beginning of the explication of the characteristics of successful high schools. Greater attention should be paid to the cultural aspects of the environment and how these can often be incongruent with each student's own culture. Also, greater attention should be paid to high schools' use of mentoring and role modeling to influence students' choice process. These are areas of research in college choice that are lacking. Another area that needs greater explication is the course-taking patterns of African American students in high school. As Pelavin and Kane's (1990) research points out, the emphasis should be on the fact that African Americans take college preparatory courses in much lower numbers than Whites. As this chapter indicates, one reason for this is teacher expectations or the culture and belief of the entire school. However, all of the responsibility does not rest with the students: a more thorough examination of this issue through the voices of principals, teachers, and students needs to occur.

In summary, there are common characteristics of high schools that are successful in channeling students to choose postsecondary education. Yet, admittedly, this is the beginning model for high schools to consider. There is more research to be conducted to explicate more conclusively how high schools can and do affect students' aspirations to attend college, particularly the characteristics of high schools that are successful in channeling their students to higher education.

CHAPTER 8

Selection of Higher Education Institution Type: HBCU or PWI?

There is much researchers know about the experiences of African Americans within different higher education institution types. Some of the well-known researchers in the field of education include Walter Allen (1992), Edgar Epps (1972), Jacqueline Fleming (1984), Michael Nettles (1988), and Reginald Wilson (1994). These scholars have written widely about the experiences of African American students attending historically Black colleges and universities (HBCUs) and predominantly White institutions (PWIs).

Curiously, less is known about the influences on African American students' choice to attend HBCUs or PWIs in the first place. In order to increase our understanding in this area, this chapter examines several questions: (1) Who and what influences the type of higher education institution African American students consider? (2) What role does cultural affinity play in the decision process for those students considering HBCUs? (3) Are students from certain high school types more likely to consider one type of higher education institution over another? The rationale for examining consideration of higher education institutional types as opposed to final selection has merit. Exploring the process and what influences these students to consider a certain type of institution can provide a much more complete range of issues for researchers and practitioners to contemplate.

First, understanding this process could provide clues concerning how to go about increasing the overall enrollment of African Americans in higher education. Next, this information could be useful to admissions officers at both HBCUs and PWIs. Many PWIs are constantly challenged with increasing their African American enrollments. Additionally, more recently, HBCUs have been seeking ways to lure the top African American high school graduates to their institutions. This is especially important in light of attempts by HBCUs to increase their enrollments (Benavides, 1996). Third, to improve retention at various higher education institutions, it is helpful to comprehend how students make their selections in the first place. Academic and social integration are more easily achieved if students are committed to the college they select to attend.

Therefore, the purpose of this chapter is to highlight a range of issues that African American students consider when choosing to attend an HBCU or PWI. Choosing between these institution types for some African American students can often be a complicated process.

African American Attendance Patterns at HBCUs and PWIs: An Overview

African American participation in higher education has been replete with struggles and triumphs. African Americans have had to struggle to gain the opportunity to participate in any form of education. As Fleming (1981) indicated, restrictive legislation was passed during the period of slavery in this country to prohibit slaves from learning to read and write. As the Civil War approached, African Americans began to realize that their best opportunity for higher education resided in establishing their own institutions. In response to this realization, African American colleges were established beginning in the 1850s (Fleming, 1981; Gurin & Epps, 1975). It is understandable, then, that late in the nineteenth and early in the twentieth century the great majority of African Americans attended historically Black colleges.

Although African Americans have had to struggle to participate in higher education, there have been triumphs. From 1850 to

1856 less than 5 percent of African Americans out of a population of 4.5 million could read and write. Since that time, African Americans have not only won their right to participate in education but have dramatically increased their enrollment in higher education from 600,000 in 1965 to 1.2 million in 1980 (Fleming, 1981; Wilson, 1994). As recently as two decades ago, the majority of African Americans in college were attending HBCUs (Wilson, 1994). African Americans were limited in their choices among types of higher education institutions. This was partially because the majority of African Americans of college age resided in the South, where segregation barriers made it impossible to select PWIs, and because admissions barriers at Northern PWIs limited access to African Americans (Gurin & Epps, 1975).

Since the 1980s, however, the change in the attendance patterns of African Americans at HBCUs and PWIs is noteworthy. Wilson (1994) describes two revolutions in federal initiatives—Supreme Court actions and congressional law—that "dramatically changed" both the number of African American participants and their geographic distribution throughout American higher education institutions. The first initiative was the passage of the GI bill, which increased by the thousands the number of African American veterans able to attend college. The second initiative was the 1964 Civil Rights Act. As a result, particularly of the 1964 Civil Rights Act, more African Americans had the opportunity to select PWIs. However, it was not until the 1970s that more African Americans began to attend PWIs, and by 1986, only 20 percent of African American students who were enrolled in higher education were attending HBCUs. In spite of these decreased numbers, HBCUs still continue to play a unique role in American higher education. These institutions have been extraordinary in their achievement of producing an overwhelming percentage of African American leaders "in the face of considerable obstacles, such as discriminatory public funding, hostility of the white power structure, low church support, [and] minimal response from the white philanthropic community and foundations" (Wilson, 1994, p. 198).

The profile of African Americans who select HBCUs has been consistent over time. In the 1970s, according to Gurin and Epps (1975), approximately 60 percent of African Americans who attended Black colleges and approximately 45 percent of African Americans who attended PWIs had fathers who had not graduated from high school. Since, according to Gurin and Epps, many African Americans' occupations have been in semiskilled or unskilled jobs, a significant difference between African Americans who selected HBCUs and those who selected PWIs was the financial support available to them. That is, according to Gurin and Epps, "Only one-third of Black students in Black colleges but one-half of those in White colleges held scholarships or grants that covered most of their college expenses" (p. 29). Therefore, the extent to which financial aid is available to African American students has likely influenced their selection of higher education institutions. Financial considerations have also tended to influence their consideration of colleges close to home. Therefore, Gurin and Epps estimated that 90 percent of students attending HBCUs in the South were Southerners.

African Americans who attend HBCUs are generally thought to have poorer high school records and lower standardized test scores than those who attend PWIs. In addition, they are generally reported to come from lower socioeconomic status families than those attending PWIs (Allen, 1992). However, Allen cautions that the assumption that PWIs provide superior environments for African American educational development is disputable. Additionally, students attending HBCUs, like students attending PWIs, have to be studied by the type of HBCU they select. There are differences among the selectivity of the colleges and the socioeconomic status of students attending different types of HBCUs (that is, private and public). Therefore, caution should be used in making general statements about the background characteristics of all students attending HBCUs.

Although in the 1980s more African Americans were electing to attend PWIs, in the 1990s, many African American students began reconsidering HBCUs because of their interest in embracing history and tradition (Benavides, 1996). Additionally, studies of African American student experiences at HBCUs and PWIs suggest that many have negative experiences at PWIs and that they suffer lower achievement and higher attrition than do White students (Allen, 1992; Nettles, 1988). In contrast, studies show that African American students who attend HBCUs experience higher intellectual gains and have more favorable psychosocial adjustment, more positive self-images, stronger racial pride, and higher aspirations (Fleming, 1984; Gurin and Epps, 1975).

In summary, while African Americans' participation in higher education has been replete with struggles and triumphs, there is still much researchers do not know about the students' decision-making process in selection of higher education institution types. What is known, according to the past research cited above, is that there was a shift in African American attendance from HBCUs to PWIs in the 1980s (Wilson, 1994).

Three Phases of the College Choice Process

Researchers who focus on college choice generally agree that the process of deciding to attend college and selecting a higher education institution falls into three phases: predisposition, search, and choice (Hossler & Gallagher, 1987; Stage & Hossler, 1989). The decision process is complicated by psychological, sociological, economic, and, previously rarely mentioned by researchers, cultural factors (characteristics unique to individuals' culture).

Hossler and Gallagher (1987) describe predisposition as the stage which has received the least amount of attention. In this stage, as has been highlighted in the previous chapters, students determine whether or not to continue their education after high school. Once the decision has been made to attend college, the search phase begins. In this second phase, students and their families begin to investigate various higher education institutions (Hanson & Litten, 1982; Hossler & Gallagher, 1987; Stage & Hossler, 1989). In the third phase, choice, students begin to narrow their options and make a final decision about which college or university to attend. Although it is useful to better understand how all three phases influence the final choice of a college, this chapter focuses on the influences on the search and choice phases.

Search Phase

During the search phase, students and higher education institutions begin to interact. Either institutions begin to woo students based on preliminary test scores, or students begin to contact institutions based on expectations they have of educational experiences. The principal sources of information about higher education as cited by high school students, according to Hanson and Litten (1982), "are college catalogs and other recruiting brochures, high school counselors, parents, peers and other friends" (p. 80). More specifically, Hanson and Litten reported that high school students discussed their post–high school plans at least three times with parents and friends. The study showed that male students had a tendency to consult fathers, and female students had a tendency to consult mothers. Further, Hanson and Litten indicated that 60 percent of the female students said that parents influenced their choice of institutional type.

As for guidance counselors, it is interesting to note that although they are influential in the predisposition stage, the findings are ambiguous regarding their influence in the final selection process (Hanson & Litten, 1982; McDonough, Antonio, & Trent, 1995). That is, according to Hanson & Litten, counselors may serve as gatekeepers, suggesting or failing to suggest higher education institutions, but may not be influential in the final selection.

How early students begin the search process also has implications for the decision process and the selection of institution type. Evidence from previous studies (Hanson & Litten, 1982; Hearn, 1991; McDonough, Antonio, & Trent, 1995) suggests that students who begin to plan for college before their senior year (as early as ninth grade) are more likely to actually matriculate than those who begin at a later time.

The studies specific to the search process for African Americans have been minimal. In their study, Hanson and Litten (1982) reported that African American students from low-income families and students whose parents have less education conduct longer, less efficient searches. They further found that these students are also more likely to rely on high school counselors for advice.

Choice Phase

Once students move through the search phase, they begin to focus on decisions related to their higher education choices. Hossler and Gallagher (1987) describe this phase as a courtship between the preferences of the applicant and the attributes of the college or university. Findings suggest that financial aid is important, particularly for African Americans (Nettles, 1988). However, for White students, there would have to be a significant increase in financial aid to cause them to move from their first choice to their second choice in schools (Hossler & Gallagher, 1987). The socio-economic composition of a secondary school tends to also influence selectivity. That is, a higher socioeconomic status of a secondary school's student body contributes to the election of more selective higher education institutions (Hanson & Litten, 1982).

The two most recent studies on African Americans as they make choices about higher education institutions were conducted by McDonough, Antonio, and Trent (1995) and Hearn, Griswold, Marine, and McFarland (1995). In the latter study, these researchers indicated that socioeconomic status (SES) and back-ground, as well as academic ability, high school track, tenth-grade expectations, and having siblings in college were positive influences on twelfth-grade expectations about college matriculation. One of their findings, which they indicate requires further study, is that the higher percentage of Whites compared to disadvantaged students as well as inequitable student-teacher and student-counselor ratios have had negative effects on African Americans' maintaining high expectations about college matriculation. These researchers further explain that "the more a school is populated by those from backgrounds socioeconomically disadvantaged in one respect or another, the more likely aspiring lower-SES students are to receive support and encouragement they need to fulfill their dreams" (pp. 15–16). McDonough, Antonio, and Trent (1995), in their quantitative study that was specific to African Americans' choosing HBCUs, suggested that the students' religion (being Baptist), the school's reputation, and relatives' desires were the top reasons the students in their sample chose to attend HBCUs. In that same study, they found that African Americans choose PWIs because they are "recruited by an athletic department, they wish to live near home, and they value the college's academic reputation" (p. 27).

Also, researchers (McDonough, Antonio, & Trent, 1995) have found that most students only apply to a small number of colleges (three or less) and that about three-quarters of them are accepted at their first-choice school. However, they also found that African American students get into their first-choice school less often than the national average. According to these researchers, on the national average approximately 70 percent of first-year students are accepted at their first-choice school, while only 55 percent of

African American students are accepted at their first-choice schools and 59 percent are accepted at their first-choice HBCUs.

These research studies on the choice process have furthered the understanding of educators and policymakers on how the majority of students decide to go to college and how they go about searching for and selecting a higher education institution to attend. Greatly understudied in all three phases of decision-making, however, is the consideration process of African American students.

Choosing an HBCU or a PWI

A clear pattern emerged in my research as I examined whether students from certain high school types were more likely to consider one type of higher education institution over another. Students who attended predominately White private high schools, in addition to considering prestigious PWIs, were also more likely to consider HBCUs than those high school students from predominately African American schools. These students described a process of searching for their roots or connection to the African American community. On the other hand, students attending predominately African American high schools strongly favored PWIs. For all students in this study, regardless of high school types, having an HBCU connection, through a family member, teacher, counselor, or friend, greatly influenced their consideration of HBCUs.

Getting Back to Their Roots

The conversations around this issue of attending HBCUs or PWIs initiated strong discussions about race relations and the pressure of being African American, particularly in private high schools. The following responses demonstrate the rationale of students attending private high schools in their consideration of HBCUs. At a private school in Chicago, a student responded:

> If you come from a White school or independent school or whatever, you want to get back with the Black people. You know, if you've been there, enough independent schools or whatever, for a long time, a lot of people want to go to Black colleges so they can go back and see their roots or whatever.

A student at a private school in New York who was planning to attend an HBCU stated:

> I'm going to feel weird being around all Black people again. It's going from all Black to White and Black and Spanish and Asian and everything and then going back to all Black again. It's just a weird transition you're going through.

Another student, attending a private school in Los Angeles, responded:

> I'm glad I've had this opportunity to come into this type of environment because when I get out into the world this is how it's going to be. I need to get used to White people and I'm glad I've had this opportunity. I wouldn't have it any other way because I do need it, especially since I'm going to a traditionally Black college.

The students who were attending independent schools stated strong feelings about what they described as "living in two different worlds." These feelings obviously led to their often being pressured by their internal communities—family, friends, and neighborhoods—to be African American, and from their external community—school—to "act White." Intense feelings were expressed about disappointment in the schools for not acknowledging their culture and history and also the responsibility of uplifting the whole race. This duality of feelings was expressed in conflicting statements regarding their consideration of higher education institution types. The students were so intense and there were so many responses on this issue that these examples only represent a few comments. All of these responses came from private school students.

Dual Life

A private school student in Los Angeles stated:

> All of my life, most of my life, until I moved here, I lived in Washington, D.C., and up until very recently, months ago, I lived in Black neighborhoods and predominately Black schools, period. I was in culture shock the first couple of months, and yeah, it's two very different worlds. Very different, not just in the color of the people, but in the way the people act.

Another private school student in Los Angeles added, "To me, it's like living a dual life. I go to school and live in a White neighborhood and all my friends are like cross-descendants. It is like living in two different worlds."

A private school student in New York said:

> So when I told my friends that I was going into private school, it was like, "Oh, my God, if you change into a White girl, I'm going to kill you." Well, that's the first thing that came into their minds. Every single one of them was like, "Oh, wait until we see you after this, you're going to be so whitewashed, it's not even funny." It was like none of them didn't even want to come up here.

A private school student in New York said, "One thing some people don't realize is that, you know, they say, 'I don't want to go to a White college or a mixed college because there's going to be too much racial tension.' There is a lot of tension that goes on." At a private school in Chicago, a student had this to say: "From here and going to a Black school is one thing because you've learned how to deal with White people already and you learn how to deal with your own people." At the same school another student said, "I think that one thing that's really beneficial about private schools is that you learn early on that there are more than just Black people in the world. That's the problem I have with Black schools, Black colleges."

Lack of Cultural Awareness

A second theme that emerged that might account for consideration of HBCUs on the part of African American students who attended private high schools related not only to their perception of the lack of knowledge White students have about the African American culture, but to their own lack of knowledge about their own culture. For example, a student attending a school in New York stated, "We have a lot of problems in that we don't really know our culture. A lot of Black people don't know where they [came] from and they don't know their culture."

Generally, students felt this lack of knowledge about their culture because classes regarding their culture were not included in the curriculum or teachers were just generally insensitive. As stated by a student attending a different private school in Chicago, "I've had a teacher tell me that I should ride the coattails of being Black: 'Don't worry about it because you have more of an advantage.' It was kind of like, 'What do you have to worry about?'—using it as an advantage. It's just something I am."

A student in Chicago responded similarly:

> I mean I'm glad that we have the choice that we can take that class, African American history, because it's taught me a lot of stuff that I probably wouldn't [have known] before. I think they can go even further with different types of Black studies.

At a private school in New York a student said, "Especially down South, I hate to say this, but for the longest time, if you are White, you are kind of like, you are better. I hate that. The Black culture is important to me."

Often when individuals are disconnected from their culture, whether through boundaries or curriculum, it is reasonable that they would have the desire to be connected or reconnected to their roots. In this sense, private and independent schools could serve as a primary thrust for HBCU recruiting.

The HBCU Connection

In addition to lack of cultural awareness, the theme of the HBCU connection emerged. As research has indicated (McDonough, Antonio, & Trent, 1995), family, teachers, and friends who have attended HBCUs greatly influence students at all high school types to consider attending HBCUs. The connection between HBCUs and their graduates continues to be strong, at least in terms of alumni desire to pass on their experiences to others. It is particularly influential for students attending private high schools.

Students across school types spoke of considering HBCUs because a family member, friend, or teacher who attended an HBCU recommended the experience. The following statements best capture the influence of family, friends, and teachers on students' consideration of HBCUs.

A student at an inner-city school in Chicago stated, "Now that I'm in high school I'm always hearing teachers, strong Black teachers,...[say that] it's mandatory that you go to an all-Black school." At another inner-city school in Chicago a student said, "I [would] rather go to a mixed college, but my counselor keeps talking about all Black colleges."

A student at a private school in Los Angeles stated:

> Like my friend—he talked about going to a Black college. I wanted to experience something new since I had been at this school for six years, and it was predominately Asian so I wouldn't mind going to a college that's all Black. My dad wants me to go to a Black college. He doesn't stress it, you know, but he wants me to go to a Black college....[You just] know he does. He doesn't want to stress it; it's up to me.

Another student attending the same school said this:

> Well, first of all, it's been a dream of my dad's ever since I've been here. I've been hearing about going to a Black college all the time. But now that I've been really thinking about it, I really want to go to a Black college because I've been in a private school all of my life, which has always been predominately White or predominately Asian or something like that. I just want to go where it's predominately Black. I just want to go somewhere where there's a majority of Black people and not be the minority of some sort.

Just as these examples from students attending a range of high schools suggest, alumni of HBCUs play a major recruiting role for HBCUs. Whether as parents, friends, teachers, or counselors, graduates of HBCUs serve as information pipelines about HBCUs for students across high school types.

The Real World Is Not Just Black

Students who attended all or predominately African American public high schools tended to view attending an HBCU from the opposite perspective of their counterparts at predominately White private high schools. They usually stated that they considered PWIs. For example, a student attending a magnet school in Washington, D.C., said, "I feel there's not an urgency to go, and, for that matter, it's not just Black and White. To be successful, you're going to have to get to know different cultures—different people with different attitudes."

A student attending a magnet school in Chicago stated, "I don't want to go to an all-Black school because I need to go to a mixed school with many cultures." At an inner-city school in Chicago, a student responded. "I want to be around people that I'm going to be around in the real world. I want to experience everything." A student at another inner-city school in Washington, D.C., said, "We should attend White colleges so Whites can understand us; so they can see we don't all stick together. Whites should see this."

It is ironic that the students who attend predominately African American high schools who consider PWIs are less likely to be recruited by these institutions.

Cultural Isolation

As a personal observation, I found that students who attended predominately African American high schools were relatively isolated from other cultural groups. Their high schools were located in predominately African American neighborhoods so that their interactions with students from other ethnic groups were particularly limited. This lack of being in a mixed environment seemed to influence their perception of the responsibility and value of sharing their culture. Therefore, their lack of interaction with Whites influenced their consideration of attending PWIs.

In summary, the considerations of higher education institution types described by the students interviewed appeared to be greatly influenced by the type of high school they attended, the type of experiences they encountered within their schools, and whether or not they had an HBCU connection through family, friends, or teachers. It is obvious from their responses that at an early age these students developed an awareness of their responsibility for projecting the whole African American race in a more positive light. These findings suggest that these feelings cut across class lines (as indicated by the type and location of schools) and school types. Students attending private high schools appeared to want to relieve themselves of this responsibility, while students attending predominately African American public high schools appeared to feel the need to take on the responsibility after being in an all-African American setting.

The Complex Process of Considering HBCUs or PWIs

It should be remembered that the majority of African Americans attending private high schools ultimately attend PWIs. It is not the intent of this chapter to dispute that fact. However, the findings from this research can inform the college choice literature in several ways. First, researching how African American students select higher education institution types provides a much more comprehensive, expansive view of the inner thinking of these students. The responses of these students demonstrate, for example, that African Americans, when making choices about the type of higher education institution to attend, generally take into account environmental issues such as their perceptions and expectations of what their experiences would be at the higher education institution. At least with this group of students, they also consider cultural factors. As pointed out in this research, students question themselves about such issues as whether it is more advantageous to be in a mixed, predominately White, or predominately Black environment.

Regarding the decision-making process concerning the type of higher education institution (HBCUs or PWIs) they would choose, these students' responses revealed the importance of exploring a wider perspective when assessing their choice of such institutions. This research seems to suggest that the more these African American students interacted with White students or attended White schools, the more likely they were to desire to "go back to their roots." On the other hand, students who had virtually no contact with other races (cultural isolation)—that is, students attending predominately African American schools—expressed the need to share their culture. It is understandable, then, that cultural awareness would be of concern to these students, a consideration not previously mentioned by college choice theorists.

It is interesting to note that students attending predominately African American high schools tended to believe that it was important to consider attending PWIs. On the other hand, it was obvious from students who attended predominately White high schools (particularly private school students) that their experiences with "lifting up the race" and the lack of cultural awareness in the curriculum led them to consider a wider band of options. Logically and intuitively, the fact that African Americans attending inner-city schools are less likely than students attending private schools to be admitted to PWIs might account for some African Americans not being accepted to their first-choice schools, as noted by McDonough, Antonio, and Trent (1995).

For admissions officers at both HBCUs and PWIs, these findings hold importance. They suggest that admissions officers at HBCUs could make better use of their alumni, teachers, and counselors at all high school types. In terms of HBCUs' use of admissions resources, these findings suggest that recruitment at private schools and other predominately White high schools might provide a good return on their investment. While the investment might not yield immediate results, it appears that over time, establishing a relationship at these schools, especially with counselors and teachers, would be beneficial in terms of having access to some of the top students. It is important to remember, at least from this research, that these students tended to express a disconnection from their culture and indicated a desire to become more culturally aware.

As for admissions officers at PWIs, establishing relationships with predominately African American high schools and students who indicate a desire to be in a mixed environment would be helpful for recruitment. When assessing the influences on these students' consideration of higher education type, it appears that there are important lessons for admissions and retention. First, while these students generally expressed the desire to select PWIs, it is important to remember that their interactions with different cultures may be limited (this in no way implies limitations on their intellect). Therefore, making the transition to a PWI could account for what students, particularly those attending predominately African American high schools, describe as experiencing culture shock. Next, having better K–12 and higher education linkages early on would be highly productive. That is particularly the case with first-generation college-goers, who could really benefit from interacting with college students and administrators so that they could obtain a more realistic picture of higher education. Also, as pointed out in this chapter, providing students with the opportunities to interact in mixed settings would be helpful.

One thing evident from this chapter is that there is a need for a greater understanding concerning the process African American students go through in their consideration of higher education institution types. My research points out that there is still much for researchers and practitioners to explore relating to how different groups decide where they want to go to college. Certainly more in-depth research needs to be conducted on each of the areas of considerations of African American students outlined in this chapter. Particularly, these findings indicate the importance of analyzing the considerations of higher education institutions by type of high school attended.

Part Three
Putting the Puzzle Together

CHAPTER 9

Students Offer Solutions

Researchers and policymakers rarely include the ideas, perceptions, or suggestions of individuals who are the focus of their studies in the development of solutions to the individuals' own problems. Although individuals or groups are often asked their opinions about their plight, they are seldom asked to participate in the development of programs or models that will improve their lives. The very individuals who would be most affected and who should be the first to be consulted are not given a voice in the dialogue, as if they had no stake in the important decisions that determine the policies that will affect the course of their lives. The process of deciding how to increase African American's participation in higher education, one of the most important commodities for upward mobility in our society, provides a prime example. African American high school students are rarely, if ever, asked for their perceptions of the problems or, more importantly, for their ideas about possible solutions.

The students in this study did not hesitate to voice their opinions about what models were needed to increase African Americans' participation in higher education—it was as though they were waiting to be asked. As evidence of the seriousness of their thoughts, it is interesting to note how their suggestions for solutions are closely aligned with their perceptions of the barriers to college attendance.

Students' comments about their perceptions of barriers to African Americans' college attendance can basically be grouped into two broad categories: economic barriers and psychological barriers (see figure 9.1). The responses relating to economic barriers can be described as a fear of either not having enough money to attend college or not getting a job that pays appropriate to the level of education after completing college. In regard to psychological barriers, which appear to pose even greater challenges to educators and policymakers, the students' responses stressed three issues: (1) college never being an option, (2) the loss of hope, and (3) the intimidation factor. The students' statements about these issues were surprisingly similar across school types, geographic regions, socioeconomic levels, and gender.

**Figure 9.1. African American High School Students'
Perceptions of Barriers to Their Participation
in Higher Education**

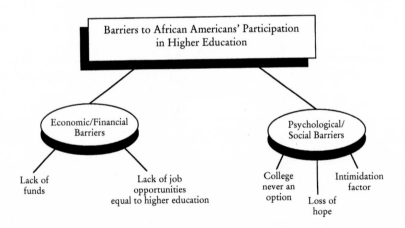

The sense of being accepted for who they are and having someone who encourages them to maximize their potential were most often stressed as being motivating factors for positive consideration of higher education. It is not surprising then that many students expressed "teaching other people about their culture" as one possible solution to increasing participation by African

American students in higher education. Another response that was frequently voiced, as pointed out in chapter 6, was having "more Black teachers—who want to be there." In fact, according to these students, what happens inside the walls of schools holds great importance for motivating African American students to seek postsecondary education.

Therefore, across school types and cities, four themes emerged from these students' suggestions concerning solutions to increase African American students' aspirations and motivation to attend college. Those mostly centered on the conditions of the place where students are being taught, who is teaching, how these teachers are teaching, and what the teachers are teaching as it relates to who these students are. Their responses can be classified into the following categories: (a) improve school conditions, (b) provide interested teachers and actively involved counselors, (c) instill possibilities early, and (d) expand cultural awareness. (See figure 9.2 for their suggestions for programs and models to increase African Americans' participation in higher education.) It is noteworthy that their suggestions closely align with the findings outlined in the other chapters in this book.

**Figure 9.2. African American High School Students'
Suggestions for Programs and Models to Increase
African Americans' Participation in
Higher Education**

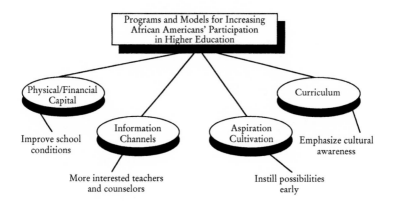

A student attending an independent school in Los Angeles captured the essence of the students' responses across cities when he stated the following:

> I think that if we were to start a program, it [should] start in the elementary school and junior high school. In my opinion, the kids would be more interested in learning; then they would want to go to college and learn more. I think that [it would help] the schools themselves in the Black neighborhoods if more money was put into them. [Then there would be] better teachers. My hat is off to teachers, but I think that teachers need to be paid more to make them want to teach more. I think that if we do that and...African Americans are [still] not excited about going to college, then we need a program...[to] upgrade and improve the schools in our neighborhoods.

Improve School Conditions

The suggestion of the need to improve the conditions of the schools was made frequently and included the need to improve the physical condition of the building as well as the contents of the building, such as providing more computers. The following statements were heard from students across both school types and cities.

An independent school student in Los Angeles said:

> My cousin...still lives in D.C., and she's still in elementary school; but for...the first three years (up to the third grade) she went to the same elementary school that I went to, and from the time I've been there until then it had just been in a steady decline. Finally, my aunt just took her out and put her in a White school. She had to either lie or pay a fine or something, but she said, "My kid can't go to this school." At this White school it's like four stories, huge and sprawling with lockers and science rooms; but in the other school it was dingy [and had] cockroaches [and] rats. She used to hate to read; she used to scream and cry when she used to have to read. Now she comes home and starts her homework. She reads for pleasure now. That's the reason why I know that if the schools were improved they would have a chance.

A student from a magnet school in Los Angeles stated:

> I know the reason why we don't have the things we need is because we are a minority school....[M]y cousin goes to another

high school and they have a computer at every desk. We have a computer lab. You have to make an appointment to go the computer lab because it's always full.

A student at an independent school in New York said, "[The] school must know what it wants to do."

Provide Interested Teachers and Actively Involved Counselors

Even more frequently stated than the need to improve schools was the suggestion that there be more interested teachers and active counselors to find ways to motivate students to participate in higher education. The students interviewed placed a greater emphasis on the value of having teachers who instill a passion in them, who believe in their ability to learn, and who push them to maximize their potential. Since this theme has been discussed in detail in chapter 7, it will not be repeated here except to reiterate the need for teachers who are interested in African American students, as well as actively involved counselors who will meet African American students' college placement needs.

Instill Possibilities Early

The idea of instilling the possibility of attending college early, as voiced by these students, included, as would be anticipated, providing information for students earlier than high school. In addition, though, the students discussed the possibility of generating excitement in the early years about higher education and the outlook for jobs after completing college. A group of students attending the same private school in New York summarized it best:

—I think what you should do [is] start really early—in third, fourth, fifth grade, whatever; get them involved in stuff that...you have to [do to] go to college to get a degree, like in communications. Give them a lot of opportunities, and in turn take them places and get them excited about [getting] out in the world and [obtaining an] education.
—Show [them] more Black people with jobs that pay who have been to college.
—Just...show people...who have been to college, Black people preferably, who have jobs that pay a lot of money, like

maybe engineers and architects. [Show them the] higher paying jobs for people who are Black.
—We have to learn how to make college seem like the best four years of your life.

A student at a magnet school in Washington, D.C., suggested, "I would tell someone in the younger age bracket to always look for a challenge, and school is always going to be a challenge."

From another perspective, an independent school student in Los Angeles concluded, "If you can show them what they can be or who is successful and how far they could really go, you know, if they do this and do that, you are already showing them a light they could try to get to."

An independent student from New York simply stated, "Invest more in younger ages."

An interesting concept concerning reaching students at an early age because of the fact that college courses cost money was stated by one suburban school student in Atlanta who warned, "[Students] just have to realize [the importance of doing well in secondary school], and they are not realizing it soon enough, because by the time they get in here they have...to pay for those classes that they didn't pass."

Additionally, an independent school student from Los Angeles stated, "I think people can be helped more when they are younger. It's hard to convince tenth or eleventh graders that never cared about college or anything."

Emphasize Cultural Awareness

During very passionate discussions about their culture, students, particularly those who attended independent high schools, voiced the need to increase cultural awareness as a way to motivate more African Americans to seek postsecondary education. Also included in this category was the need for more male role models. A student at an independent school in Los Angeles said, "We need more Black male role models." An independent school student in New York said there was a need for

more role models that don't play sports all the time. I mean I love them, I love basketball, but we need to get kids at a young age to love education and to feel the need that they have to do this to survive in the world because, without it, you're just going to be like lost.

Within their communities across cities, particularly at private (primarily White) high schools, students indicated tremendous pressure to be accepted, describing the feeling of "living in two different worlds." Several students described their experiences of having Black friends in their communities accuse them of "acting White" because they attended private predominately White high schools, and they felt the pressure of being accepted in the school environment by Whites.

Students' Thoughts Should Be a Part of the Solution

This chapter points out the importance of researchers not only including individuals as subjects in their studies but also including their voices in the development of solutions to their problems. That is particularly the case when studies cut across cultures. As in the case of this study, while student choice and economics of education theorists have long documented the influences on the decision-making process for students (see the theoretical perspectives discussed throughout this book), one explanation for the failure of models and programs to increase African Americans' participation in higher education could be a lack of understanding of what the influences mean in the context of the African American culture.

For example, my research does not disagree with student choice theorists' findings that indicate the importance of parental education and income. However, when these students describe barriers and possible solutions to African American college attendance, they look to the importance of the primary and secondary schools and their teachers, counselors, and programs to prepare students for higher education. Understanding this in the context of the African American culture has merit. The school system plays an even greater role when parents themselves have not attended college, as many of the students in this sample came from homes where neither parent had done so.

However, it should not be concluded that students who do not live in the traditional two-parent family, particularly in the inner city, are not aware of the value of higher education. My research suggests that while these students are aware of the barriers to

African Americans' access to higher education, they nonetheless still perceive that it is worth the cost. Therefore, researchers should use caution in interpreting lack of information as lack of interest. In fact, these students offered viable options for ways of increasing the information channels.

As indicated by these students, it has become increasingly clear that the information pipeline to students, particularly to those students who do not have the intergenerational benefit of having higher education passed down to them, must begin much earlier, and it must be incorporated in some structured format within the primary and secondary schools, especially public schools. It is in this way, as Orfield et al. (1984) have suggested, that channeling can improve the choice process for students.

The students in this study appeared to be stressing more than a lack of information when they discussed instilling possibilities early. Rather, it could be concluded that these students were saying that if schools are not going to provide information through teachers and counselors, then, at a minimum, educators should not take away students' passion by instilling in them what they cannot be. This interpretation would support these students' perceived psychological barriers of loss of hope and feeling that college was never an option. It is here that the research on social and cultural capital can shed light for educators on how students perceive that they are not provided a passion to participate in higher education. It is through the concept of cultural capital, as defined by Bourdieu and Passeron (1977), that educators have already established views of what is acceptable behavior, typically based on the majority culture. In public school settings where students do not meet those established views, educators begin early on the process of stripping away cultural values which could, as these students describe, leave students feeling hopeless and passionless.

Given these realities, it is understandable, then, that these students would echo the importance of emphasizing cultural awareness. This aspect of their model (see figure 9.2) is one that student choice and economics of education theorists have not explored and that merits much greater understanding. What exactly is the role that increasing cultural awareness in the curriculum at the earliest possible age plays in increasing students' participation in higher education? According to these students, at a minimum, it would improve their sense of self and instill a passion for learning. While Ogbu (1988) has written about the burden of acting White, these students appeared to be saying that this is just the reality of being African American in America. That is, instead of feeling as though their "acting White" is a negative statement about their culture, it could be interpreted to mean that if their culture were more inclusive in the curriculum and other aspects of the American society, they could be themselves across settings as opposed to having to leave their culture behind within their communities.

Along with cultural awareness, this research demonstrates that, at least in this sample, students' views cut across class lines. This finding provides impetus for the growing notion that cultural views (that is, behaviors, values, and frames of reference) outweigh class differences.

It would seem logical, then, that African Americans, and in this case high school students, are in the best place to assist educators and policymakers in the development of solutions for increasing African Americans' participation in higher education. This book poses some challenging questions for policymakers: In the absence of parental influence on students' post–high school plans, what are ways of including African American students in decision making regarding their lives? What different roles can K–12 and postsecondary schools play in addressing students' concerns related to cultural considerations? How should educators address these students' concerns about the psychological barriers that they perceive Africans Americans face in making college choices? How can educators and policymakers address these students' fear of not achieving future earnings appropriate to their level of education after completing higher education?

Although rarely asked their opinions, this chapter demonstrates that these students tended to voice concerns and solutions that could possibly impact the course of college choice for African Americans in general. Workable solutions have to come from the sources most familiar with their circumstances. There is great reason for optimism, however. Based on the extensive research that student choice and economics of education theorists have carried out on the college choice process, the development of models and programs to increase African American students' motivation and aspiration to participate in higher education is within reach. This book points out that the missing link to previous research has been the voices of the students. The next step is for educators and policymakers to work with African American students, to empower them, to more formally investigate their thoughts, and to develop sites to test their model.

It is clear that current models are not working, and these students' ideas are solid ones. It would be difficult to find anyone who would disagree that physical and financial resources are necessary for inner-city schools, that interested teachers and actively involved counselors are needed, that instilling possibilities earlier is a necessity, and, across all school types, that having a curriculum that is inclusive of all cultures (not just during one event or one month) is desperately lacking.

However, all too often, researchers unfamiliar with the historical and structural differences of cultures continue to both define the problems and develop solutions based on models that are applicable to the majority population. In order to develop workable programs and models, educators and policymakers must begin the process of hearing the voices that are all too often relegated to the margins, for, logically and intuitively, those are the only voices that can possibly hold the solutions.

CHAPTER 10

The Case for Expanding the College Choice Model

As pointed out in this book, the Hossler and Gallagher (1987) model needs to be greatly expanded to include cultural characteristics. Since it is widely accepted (and further demonstrated in this book) that family and schools play a major role in influencing students' aspirations and motivations to participate in higher education, the individual and collective roles that each plays are crucial for African American students.

To merely indicate that significant others or more specifically parents influence college choice is not enough. How the process works has to be understood in order to effect change. For example, in every culture, because of historical and environmental circumstances, the family structure (whether single, dual, or extended) has to be studied and programs or models developed based on the uniqueness of each cultural group. To develop models based on one culture (for example, the Hossler and Gallagher model) does not allow for differences in the way that families influence their children's college choice process.

Also, better understanding how schools influence different cultural groups' aspirations and motivations to choose higher education is a necessity. For example, as this book suggests, African American students perceive that school (at the elementary and secondary levels) impacts their choice process both negatively and positively, depending on how the students and their culture are viewed by the school. As such, in order for workable programs and models to be developed to increase the aspirations and motivation of African American students, the role of the school in that process has to be examined in much greater detail. Particularly, it is important to not just focus on programs that are not successful in influencing college choice positively, but to examine the characteristics of schools that are successful in channeling students to participate in higher education, as outlined in chapter 7.

Additionally, new and different aspects of school culture must be examined as they relate to college choice. For example, as chapter 5 suggests, the curriculum, which is the heart and soul of a school, must be better understood and added to the model. Another question that college choice theorists must begin to focus on is how families and schools can work together more closely to influence the choice process of seekers and dreamers, the types of students described in chapter 2. As many African American students are still first-generation college-goers, in order to influence the college attendance rate of these students, these are the categories of students whose college choices must be impacted.

However, it is clear that the voices of African American students and parents must be heard. As the previous chapter noted, African American students are well aware of their circumstances and have given thought to possible solutions. It is terribly unfortunate that they and their parents are rarely asked about their opinions. Since this book focuses on the voices of African American students, a similar study that includes the parents' perceptions of the ways they influence the college choice process of their children would be enormously beneficial.

In thinking about ways to put pieces of this puzzle together (that is, why African American students have the highest aspiration to participate in higher education but often do not act on their aspiration), I would like to offer an expanded version of the Hossler and Gallagher (1987) model as it relates to predetermination, phase one of the college choice process. First, in my model, (see figure 10.1) I refer to phase one of the college decision-making process as "predetermination." I do so because environmental circumstances often have much to do with whether students will choose higher education. In that sense, the decision is often predetermined by the circumstances outside of the students' control, as chapter 6 shows.

Figure 10.1. Model of Predetermination

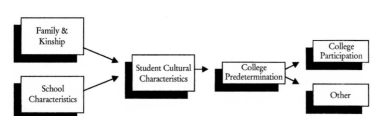

Next, as demonstrated in figure 10.1, family and kinship and school characteristics must be funneled through students' cultural characteristics in order to understand the influences on students' college choice. This model, then, differs from Hossler and Gallagher's because their model does not take into account students' cultural characteristics. Also, my model differs from theirs in the subcategories that my research suggests should be included under the categories of "family and kinship" and "school characteristics." As suggested, under "family and kinship," who influences students and how they are influenced must be studied, and under "school characteristics" the curriculum and the time frame of the decision-making process must be examined in much greater detail.

One thing that is clear from this book is that to interpret why African American students have the highest stated aspiration to participate in higher education among all groups and yet their actual participation does not match their stated interest, the influence of family and school upon the decision process must be better understood. However, the interpretation of any findings absent an understanding of a group's culture is analogous to attaching wings to a turtle and then being perplexed as to why the turtle cannot fly. This analogy is the best rationale for the need to expand the college choice model, particularly phase one, predetermination.

APPENDIX

Design of the Study

To investigate the questions raised in this study, a qualitative inquiry method using groups was utilized. Why the qualitative approach? The voices of students are rarely heard in the debates regarding their lives, and the voices of disempowered students are even more silent, as stated by Nieto (1992). The purpose of this approach—using group interviews—was to allow a greater and more diverse number of African American students a voice and thus to provide a deeper understanding of their consideration of the value of higher education. According to Nieto, qualitative studies can enable us to examine "particular situations so that solutions can be hypothesized and developed" (p. 5).

Data Collection Procedures

The data for this research were gathered through structured group interviews. A protocol was developed for the interviews based on pilot testing of a survey that was administered to a sampling of students in an inner-city school and in a private school in Atlanta, Georgia. (Atlanta was selected as a test site because of convenience of location.) After reviewing the responses on the survey, the researcher was left with many unanswered questions. The students' write-in responses indicated a desire to explain their answers further, and therefore group interviews, as outlined by

Nieto, were determined to be an effective means of hearing students' voices.

Although there was a formal protocol, the interviews and guiding questions were generally flexible and informal in order to allow students to express their issues and concerns more freely. For better control of reliability in the questioning process, the researcher personally conducted all of the focus group interviews. The interviews were audiotaped, and the tapes were transcribed by a professional transcriber. The data were reread several times to confirm coding.

Primary patterns and themes in the interview transcripts were evaluated based on procedures outlined in Miles and Huberman (1984), who explain that "pattern codes are explanatory or inferential codes, ones that identify an emergent theme, pattern, or explanation" (p. 67), and further, that "the bedrock of inquiry is the researcher's quest for repeatable regularities" (p. 67). The data were analyzed using what Miles and Huberman refer to as a "start list," a deductive approach and cross-group analysis. A master list of codes was developed around the conceptual framework, the pilot test, and the research questions using general categories with descriptive marginal remarks. Based on the master codes, cross-group analysis was used to determine commonality in themes and patterns among the responses of the different groups.

Student and Site Selection

Focus group sessions were conducted in each of five cities that have large African American populations: Atlanta, Chicago, Los Angeles, New York, and Washington, D.C. These cities were selected based on the previous work of Neimi (1975) and Simms (1995). Both indicated that these cities have the largest cross section of African American populations, and Simms further noted that they are among the metropolitan cities where African Americans have the highest median income and lowest poverty rates.

Group interviews included African American students (male and female) in tenth, eleventh, and twelfth grades. These grades were the focus of this study because it is typically in these grades that students have already formed their perceptions about the worth of the investment in postsecondary education. In order to ensure a cross section of school types, students in inner-city, sub-urban, magnet, and private schools in these cities were included. As a first step, school board administrators in each city were asked to recommend schools based on the researcher's request for the stated school types. In each school, the principal or headmaster selected the group participants based on criteria the researcher outlined: all African Americans and equal numbers by gender, grade, and socioeconomic background (particularly in private schools). It is often difficult to gain access to private schools to conduct research. Therefore, when this study was given the support of the National Association of Independent Schools, it was decided to oversample private schools to obtain as much research data as possible from this school type. In addition, the researcher wanted to assess the differences in responses to the research questions by African American students from different socioeconomic levels. Such a cross section of schools, particularly private schools with African American students, would be inclusive of a broader range of socioeconomic levels.

A total of seventy students participated in sixteen group interviews. The breakdown by school, gender, and grade is noted in table 1. In the inner-city school in New York and in one of the inner-city schools in Washington, D.C., interviews were conducted with two small classes. In each case, one class was college preparatory and one class was not college bound. Because these classes were much larger than the groups, the numbers are not included in the total participant numbers in table 1. However, the responses of students from these classes were coded and are included in the analysis. In group analysis, it is acceptable to include these responses because the study was designed to find patterns and themes based on the theoretical framework and the research questions. Though it is recognized that there is an uneven distribution of school types across cities, the diversity and the number of schools and students participating in the study allowed a representative sampling.

The background of the students varied, but there were some commonalities. In most cases, across school types, the students were first-generation college-goers—most were from homes where the parents did not attend college. Though students were not asked any questions about income because the researcher's interest was in

Table A-1
Profile of School Participants in African American High School Focus Groups

School Type	School Location	No. of Schools	Participants	Gender		Grade Level		
				Male	Female	12th	11th	10th
Inner-City	Chicago	2						
	School A		2	1	1	1	1	0
	School B		4	2	2	3	1	0
	New York*							
	Washington, D.C.	2						
	School A		3	0	3	1	0	2
	School B*							
Magnet	Chicago	1	6	3	3	3	3	0
	Los Angeles	1	4	1	3	1	3	0
	Washington, D.C.	1	5	2	3	3	0	2
Private	Atlanta	1	5	3	2	5	0	0
	Chicago	2						
	School A		6	3	3	5	1	0
	School B		7	3	4	3	2	2
	Los Angeles	2						
	School A		5	2	3	2	2	1
	School B		5	2	3	1	2	2
	New York	2						
	School A		6	1	5	3	2	1
	School B		5	2	3	0	0	5
Suburban	Atlanta	1	7	6	1	7	0	0
		16	70	31	39	38	17	15

* At the request of school officials, classes were interviewed as groups; therefore the number of individual participants is not relevant to this table.

the students' responses in the aggregate, the school distribution provided a basis for assumptions about income level. That is, it would not be expected that the income of parents of students who attended inner-city schools would be as high as that of parents of students who attended private schools. It is important to note, however, that several African American students in private schools were on scholarships.

Data Analysis

As a result of the pilot test, it was decided that the best way to examine students' perceptions of the value of higher education was to ask questions in a way that was not specific to their own college plans. One of the high school principals said that American society places so much emphasis on higher education that for students to answer that they do not plan to attend college or that they do not perceive higher education to be worth the cost automatically makes them feel as if they are failures. Martin Carnoy of Stanford University (personal communication, 1991) indicated that if the question is made specific to the student, the student's response might imply that higher education is worth the investment, but "for other people, not me."

Thus, to encourage students to express their perceptions of the barriers (costs) to African Americans' participation in higher education, my question to them was, "Will you help me to better understand why there seems to be a lack of interest among African American high school graduates regarding participation in higher education?" In this way, students could more freely describe the barriers they perceived. This guiding question also served the twofold purpose of eliciting not only statements of barriers to participation but also expressions of student-perceived solutions to these barriers. Themes were developed from the most frequently stated responses by the students. As Levine and Nidiffer (1996) noted about the findings from the interviews of their subjects, "When asked how they came to attend college, each of them told almost the same story" (p. 65). Although the students in this sampling attended different school types and lived in different geographic regions, their responses varied little.

REFERENCES

Alexander, K., D'Amico, R., Fennessey, J., & McDill, E. (1978). *Status composition and educational goals: An attempt at clarification.* Report 244. Baltimore: Johns Hopkins University Center for Social Organizations of Schools.

Allen, W. (1992). The color of success: African American college student outcomes at predominately White and historically Black colleges. *Harvard Educational Review, 6*(2), 26–44.

Allen, W., & Epps, E. (1991). *College in Black and White: African American students in predominately White and historically Black public universities.* Albany: State University of New York Press.

Alwin, D. F., & Otto, L. B. (1977, October). High school context effects on aspiration. *Sociology of Education, 50*, 259–273.

American Association of University Women (AAUW). (1990). *How schools shortchange girls.* Washington, DC.: Author.

Anderson, J. D. (1988). *Education of Blacks in the South: 1860–1935.* Chapel Hill: University of North Carolina Press.

Anderson, M., & Hearn, J. (1992). Equity issues in higher education outcomes. In W. E. Becker & D. R. Lewis (Eds.), *The economics of American higher education* (pp. 301–334). Norwell, MA: Kluwer Academic.

Aptheker, H. (Ed.). (1973). *The education of Black people: Ten critiques, 1906–1960 by W. E. B. DuBois.* New York: Monthly Review Press.

Arnold, K. (1996). The fulfillment of promise: Minority valedictorians and salutatorians. In F. K. Stage, G. L. Araya, J. P. Bean, D. Hossler, and G. D. Kreh (Eds.), *College students: The evolving nature of research* (ASHE Reader Series, pp. 84–99). Needham, MA: Simon & Schuster.

Banks, J. A. (1988). *Multiethnic education* (2nd ed.). Boston: Allyn and Bacon.

Barnes, A. S. (1992). *Retention of African American males in high school.* New York: University Press of America.

Bateman, M., & Hossler, D. (1996). Exploring the development of postsecondary education plans among African American and White students. *College and University, 72*(1), 2–9.

Becker, G. S. (1975). *Human capital* (2nd ed.). New York: Columbia University Press.

Benavides, I. (1996, February 19). Historically Black colleges buying muscle to up enrollment. *The Tennessean,* IA.

Billingsley, A. (1992). *Climbing Jacob's ladder: The enduring legacy of African-American families.* New York: Simon & Schuster.

Bourdieu, P., & Passeron, P. (1977). *Reproduction in education, society and culture.* London: Sage.

Boyer, E. (1987). *College: The undergraduate.* New York: Harper & Row.

Boyle, R. (1966). The effect of the high school on students' aspirations. *The American Journal of Sociology, 6,* 628–639.

Brown, M. C. (1999). *The quest to define collegiate desegregation: Black colleges, Title VI compliance, and post-Adams litigation.* Westport, CT: Bergin & Garvey.

Brown, M. C. (2000). Prophets of power in the professoriate: A sermon for cultural workers. In M. C. Brown & J. E. Davis (Eds.), *Black sons to mothers: Compliments, critiques, and challenges for cultural workers in education* (pp. 219–234). New York: Peter Lang.

Brown, M. C. (2002). Equity and access in higher education: Changing the definition of educational opportunity. *Readings on Equal Education, 18.* New York: AMS Press.

Brown, M. C., & Bartee, R. D. (2000). African-American students within the desegregated p-16 pipeline: Opportunities, outcomes, and value-based ideologies. *National Alliance of Black School Educators Journal, 4,* 15–25.

Brown, M. C., & Davis, J. E. (2000). To be or not to be a mother: Introducing the conversation. In M. C. Brown & J. E. Davis (Eds.), *Black sons to mothers: Compliments, critiques, and challenges for cultural workers in education* (pp. 1–12). New York: Peter Lang.

Carnoy, M. (1995). *Faded dreams: The politics and economics of race in America.* New York: Cambridge University Press.

Carter, D., & Wilson, R. (Eds.). (1993). *Status of minorities in higher education.* Washington, DC: American Council on Education.

Carter, D., & Wilson, R. (Eds.). (1994). *Status of minorities in higher education.* Washington, DC: American Council on Education.

Carter, D., & Wilson, R. (Eds.). (1995). *Status of minorities in higher education.* Washington, DC: American Council on Education.

Chapman, D. W. (1981). A model of student college choice. *Journal of Higher Education, 52*(5), 490–505.

Cicourel, A. V., & Mehan, H. (1985). Universal development, stratifying practices, and status attainment. *Research in Social Stratification and Mobility, 4*(5), 728–734.

Cohn, E. (1979). *The economics of education.* Cambridge: Harper & Row.

Coleman, J. S. (1988). Social capital in the creation of human capital. *American Journal of Sociology, 94,* 95–120.

Coleman, J. S. (1990). *Foundations of social theory.* Cambridge: Belknap Press of Harvard University.

Collins, R. (1979). *The credential society: An historical sociology of education and stratification.* San Diego: Academic Press.

Comer, J. P., & Poussaint, A. F. (1992). *Raising Black children: Two leading psychiatrists confront the educational, social, and emotional problems facing black children.* New York: Plume.

Cross, P., & Astin, H. (1981). Factors affecting Black students' persistence in college. In G. Thomas (Ed.), *Black students in higher education* (pp. 76–90). Westport, CT: Greenwood Press.

Cuyjet, M. J. (1997). African American men on college campuses: Their needs and their perceptions. *New Directions for Student Services, 80,* 5–16.

De Castell, S., & Bryson, M. (Ed.). (1997). *Radical in(ter)ventions: Identity, politics, and difference/s in educational praxis.* Albany: State University of New York Press.

Delpit, L. (1995). *Other people's children: Cultural conflict in the classroom*. New York: New Press.

deMarrais, K. B., & LeCompte, M. D. (1998). *The way schools work: A sociological analysis of education* (3rd ed.). New York: Longman.

DiMaggio, P., & Mohr, J. (1985). Cultural capital, educational attainment, and marital selection. *American Journal of Sociology, 90*(6), 1231–1261.

Ellsworth, G., Day, N., Hurworth, R., & Andrews, J. 1982. *From high school to tertiary study: Transition to college and university in Victoria*. Hawthorn, Victoria: Australian Council for Educational Research.

Epps, E. G. (1972). Higher education and Black Americans: Implications for the future. In E. G. Epps (Ed.), *Black students in White schools* (pp. 102–111). Worthington, OH: Charles A. Jones.

Feagans, V. (1997). *The perils of school: Cultural clashes in communities and classroom*. New York: Columbia University Press.

Feagin, J. R., Vera, H., & Imani, N. (1996). *The agony of education: Black students at White colleges and universities*. New York: Routledge.

Fleming, J. (1984). *Blacks in college*. San Francisco: Jossey-Bass.

Fleming, J. H. (1981). Blacks in higher education to 1954: A historical overview. In G. E. Thomas (Ed.), *Black students in higher education: Conditions and experiences in the 1970s* (pp. 11–17). Westport, CT: Greenwood Press.

Foster, M. (1997). *Black teachers on teaching*. New York: New Press.

Franklin, J. H., & Lightfoot, S. L. (1989). *Visions of a better way: A Black appraisal of public schooling*. Washington, DC: Joint Center for Political Studies.

Freeman, K. (1997). Increasing African Americans' participation in higher education: African American high school students' perspective. *Journal of Higher Education, 68*(5), 523–550.

Gurin, P., & Epps, E. G. (1975). *Black consciousness, identity, and achievement: A study of students in historically Black colleges*. New York: Wiley.

Hamrick, F. A., & Stage, F. K. (1998). High minority enrollment, high school lunch rates: Predisposition to college. *Review of Higher Education, 21*(4), 343–357.

Hanson, K. H., & Litten, L. H. (1989). Mapping the road to academe: A review of research on women, men, and the college-selection process. In P. J. Perun (Ed.), *The undergraduate woman: Issues in educational equity* (pp. 73–98). Lexington, MA: Lexington Books.

Hearn, J. C. (1991). Academic and nonacademic influences on the college destinations of 1980 high school graduates. *Sociology of Education, 64,* 158–171.

Hearn, J. C., Griswold, C. P., Marine, G. M., & McFarland, M. L. (1995). *Dreams realized and dreams deferred: A causal analysis of six years of educational expectations and attainment.* Paper presented at the 1996 meeting of the American Educational Research Association, New York.

Hollins, E. R. (1996). *Culture in school: Revealing the deeper meaning.* Mahway, NJ: Erlbaum.

Hossler, D., Braxton, J., & Coopersmith, G. (1989). Understanding student college choice. In J. C. Smart (Ed.), *Higher education: Handbook of theory and research* (Vol. 5, pp. 231–288). New York: Agathon Press.

Hossler, D., & Gallagher, K. (1987). Studying student college choice: A three-phase model and the implications for policymakers. *College University, 62*(3), 207–221.

Hossler, D., Schmit, J., & Vesper, N. (1999). *Going to college: How social, economic, and educational factors influence the decisions students make.* Baltimore: Johns Hopkins University.

Hossler, D., & Vesper, N. (1993). *Consistency and change in college matriculation decisions: An analysis of the factors which influence the college selection decisions of students.* Paper presented at the meeting of the American Educational Research Association, Atlanta, GA.

Irvine, J. J. (1990). *Black students and school failure: Policies, practices, and prescriptions.* Westport, CT: Praeger.

Johns, R. L., Morphet, E. L., & Alexander, K. (1983). *The economics and financing of education* (4th ed.). Englewood Cliffs, NJ: Prentice-Hall.

King, J. E. (1995). Culture-centered knowledge: Black studies, curriculum transformation, and social action. In J. Banks & C. A. Banks (Eds.), *Handbook of research on multicultural education*. New York: Macmillan.

Ladson-Billings, G. (1994). *The dreamkeepers: Successful teachers of African American children*. San Francisco: Jossey-Bass.

Levine, A., & Nidiffer, J. (1996). *Beating the odds: How the poor get to college*. San Francisco: Jossey-Bass.

Lewis, S. A. R. (1997). The family, the church, and the historically Black college: Institutions of achievement for the Black community. In F. T. Trotter (Ed.), *Politics, morality, and higher education: Essays in honor of Samuel DuBois Cook*. Franklin, TN: Providence House.

Litten, L., Sullivan, D., & Brodigan, D. (1983). *Applying market research in college admissions*. New York: The College Board.

London, H. B. (1992). Transformation: Cultural challenges faced by first-generation students. In L. S. Zwerling & H. B. London (Eds.), *First-generation students: Confronting the cultural issues* (pp. 5-11). San Francisco: Jossey-Bass.

McDonough, P. (1994, July/August). Buying and selling higher education: The social construction of the college applicant. *Journal of Higher Education, 65*(4), 427–446.

McDonough, P., Antonio, A., & Trent, J. (1995). *Black students, Black colleges: An African American college choice model*. Paper presented at the meeting of the American Educational Research Association, San Francisco.

Mickelson, R. A. (1990). The attitude-achievement paradox among Black adolescents. *Sociology of Education, 63*, 44–61.

Miles, M. B., & Huberman, A. M. (1984). *Qualitative data analysis*. Newbury Park, CA: Sage.

Morgan, H. (1995). *Historical perspectives on the education of Black children*. Westport, CT: Praeger.

Morrison, L. (1989). The Lubin House experience: A model for the recruitment and retention of urban minority students. In J. C. Elam (Ed.), *Blacks in higher education: Overcoming the odds* (pp. 11–27). New York: University Press of America.

Mortenson, T. (1991). *Equity of higher educational opportunity for women, Black, Hispanic, and low income students*. Iowa City, IA: American College Testing Program.

Nettles, M. (1988). *Financial aid and minority participation in graduate education.* Princeton, NJ: Minority Graduate Education Project for Educational Testing Service.

Nettles, M. (Ed.). (1988). *Toward Black undergraduate student equity in American Higher education.* Westport, CT: Greenwood Press.

Niemi, A. W. (1975, January). Racial differences in returns to educational investment in the South. *American Journal of Economics and Sociology, 34,* 87–94.

Nieto, S. (1992). *Affirming diversity: The sociopolitical contest of multicultural education.* White Plains, NY: Longman.

Ogbu, J. U. (1978). *Minority education and caste.* New York: Academic Press.

Ogbu, J. U. (1988). Cultural diversity and human development. In T. Slaughter (Ed.), *Black children and poverty: A developmental perspective* (pp. 11–27). San Francisco: Jossey-Bass.

Orfield, G. (1992). Money, equity, and college access. *Harvard Educational Review, 62*(3), 337–371.

Orfield, G., Mitzel, H., Austin, T., Bentley, R., Bice, D., Dwyer, M., et al. (1984). *The Chicago study of access and choice in higher education* (Report prepared for the Illinois Senate Committee on Higher Education). Chicago: Illinois Senate Committee.

Pelavin, S. H., & Kane, M. (1990). *Changing the odds: Factors increasing access to college.* New York: College Entrance Examination Board.

Perlman, R. (1973). *The economics of education: Conceptional problems and policy issues.* New York: McGraw-Hill.

Schmidt, P., & Hossler, D. (1995). *Where are they now?: A nine year longitudinal study of student college choice.* Paper presented at the American Educational Research Association Annual Meeting, San Francisco, CA.

Schultz, T. W. (1961). Investment in human capital. *American Economic Review, 51,* 1–17.

Shujaa, M. (Ed.). (1994). *Too much schooling, too little education: A paradox of Black life in White societies.* Trenton, NJ: Africa World Press.

Simms, M. (1995, July). The place to be: Washington. *Black Enterprise, 24.*

Stage, F., & Hossler, D. (1989). Differences in family influences on college attendance plans for male and female ninth graders. *Research in Higher Education, 30*(3), 301–315.

St. John, E. P. (1991). What really influences minority attendance?: Sequential analyses of the high school and beyond sophomore cohort. *Research in Higher Education, 32*(2), 141–158.

Swartz, E. (1996). Emancipatory narratives: Rewriting the master script in the school curriculum. In M. F. Rogers (Ed.) & G. Ritzer (Consulting Ed.), *Multicultural experiences, multicultural theories* (pp. 164–176). New York: McGraw-Hill.

Thomas, G. E. (1980). Race and sex differences and similarities in the process of college entry. *Higher Education, 9,* 179–202.

Thurow, L. C. (1972). Education and economic equality. *Public Interest, 28,* 66–81.

Tuttle, R. (1981). *A path analytical model of the college going decision* (Tech. Rep. ED 224 434). Boone, NC: Appalachian State University.

Walker, V. S. (1996). *Their highest potential: An African American school community in the segregated south.* Chapel Hill: University of North Carolina.

Washington, B. T. (1989). *Up from slavery.* Secaucus, NJ: First Carol Publishing Group.

Watkins, W. H., Lewis, J. H., and Chou, V. (2001). *Race and educations: The roles of history and society in educating African American students.* Boston: Allyn & Bacon.

Wilson, K. R., & Allen, W. R. (1987). Explaining the educational attainment of young Black adults: Critical familial and extra-familial influences. *Journal of Negro Education, 56*(1), 64–76.

Wilson, R. (1994). The participation of African Americans in American higher education. In M. J. Justiz, R. Wilson, & L. G. Bjork (Eds.), *Minorities in higher education* (pp. 195–211). Phoenix, AZ: Oryx Press.

INDEX

Part One
Familial and Individual Influences

3 1833 04818 9390